$TOP

LIVING

PAYCHECK-TO-PAYCHECK

The **Rainy Day Guide** to Saving Cash,
Drowning Debt and Creating More
FINANCIAL FREEDOM

(How I **Saved $100k** in 12 Months)

MICHELLE KULP

This book is designed to provide accurate and authoritative information in regard to the subject matter herein. It is sold with the understanding that the author and publisher is not engaged in rendering legal, accounting, or other professional services. If you require legal advice or other expert assistance, you should seek the services of a competent professional.

While the author has made every effort to provide accurate website addresses and other information at the time of publication, neither the publisher nor the author assumes any responsibility for errors or changes that occur after publication. Further, the publisher does not have any control over and does not assume any responsibility for author or third-party websites or their content.

"You must gain control over your money or the lack of it will forever control you." *~Dave Ramsey*

"Surprise expenses will always crop up, no matter how thoroughly you plan." *~Karen McCall, Founder of the Financial Recovery Institute, and author of "Financial Recovery"*

"The thing money gives you is the freedom not to worry about money." *~Johnny Carson*

"Stop settling for less and start opting for more."
~Barbara Stanny, author of Secrets of Six-Figure Women

"We think that if we can just work harder, longer, better – if we can just hold out – something good will happen one day. Something big is just around the corner, right? Something just like magic will wipe away all of the debt, financial stress, and worry. After all, don't we deserve that? Isn't that how the story is supposed to end? No, my friend, that happens only in the movies – nothing like we experience in real life."
~Mike Michalowicz, Author of Profit First: Transform Your Business From a Cash-Eating Monster to a Money-Making Machine

TABLE OF CONTENTS

INTRODUCTION

One year ago, I had exactly zero money in my savings account and was living paycheck-to-paycheck.

12 months later, I had $100k in my savings account.

So, what transpired during that time that led to these remarkable results? No, I didn't win the lottery or receive an unexpected windfall.

I have been a six-figure income earner for many years. So it wasn't about my level of income. You can be a high income earner and still be living paycheck-to-paycheck. I used to joke to family and friends, *"I'm great at making money, just not very good at managing money."*

A year ago, I was looking at my life and felt there were some emotional blocks preventing me from living life at my full potential in a few areas. Consequently, I attended an emotional healing retreat and it was transformational. Many of my money issues were coming from my subconscious and emotional blocks as well as my mindset.

What happened after that was nothing short of miraculous. It was like the floodgates opened up and I started attracting higher-level clients. I also teamed up with a great business partner to offer a new high-ticket package and signed several new clients into that program.

After I did this deep emotional healing, my income soared and instead of spending everything I was earning, I made the conscious and intentional decision NOT to live on the financial edge any more.

My first goal was simply to have at least three months of living expenses in savings. I didn't want to burden my family if, for some reason, I was unable to pay my bills. I wrote down my goal and started saving more and spending less. I was not living in total deprivation mode either (I drive a Lexus, eat out frequently and go to Starbucks), but I was doing a lot less unconscious spending. At the same time, my income began to increase exponentially.

Within a few months, I had achieved my first goal and felt very proud of myself. I then decided my next goal was to have six months of living expenses in the bank; so I repeated what I was already doing and in the next few months, I saved a total of six months' living expenses. I continued doing this until after 12 months, I had saved $100k in the bank.

My living expenses are about $4k per month; so if something were to happen and I couldn't work, I would still be able to pay my living expenses for two years.

I actually turned saving money into a game and it was super fun to see my savings account increase every month. I didn't have a lot of debt because several years ago during the real estate crash, I sold my million-dollar house at a short sale. I didn't have many credit cards because the short sale caused my credit score to drop from 740 to 535. What little debt I had, I was able to eliminate.

In Chapter 6, I'll explain how I increased my credit score from 535 to 800+ in all three credit bureaus. I'll also teach you how to play the credit game.

I am not a financial planner; I do not have a degree in accounting. I did, however, have a 17-year career as a paralegal, so I have developed a skillset that allows me to think strategically and become very laser focused once I set my mind to something.

After my paralegal career ended in 2000, I transitioned into outside sales and in 2004, I started making six figures. I worked in outside sales for 10 years until the real estate crash which caused the company I was working for to file for bankruptcy.

I started my first website (becomea6figurewoman.com) in 2005 and created a new part-time income stream selling online courses. Since I was earning six figures at my outside sales job, I wasn't 100% focused on my part-time online business. However, when my sales job was eliminated, I had to figure out how to turn my side hustle into my full-time hustle.

With the help of an amazing business coach, I turned my business around from making a few thousand a month to making $20k+ per month. My 6-figure online business is www.bestsellingauthorprogram.com.

I love what I do! I am passionate about books. I've written over 10 of my own (I'm writing a book a month in 2020) and I've helped over 200 authors publish, launch and become #1 bestselling authors! Books are my life!

I am writing this book because I know it will help others who may have a similar story. Maybe you're a great income earner and a terrible money manager, or maybe you have some emotional blocks and are self-sabotaging yourself. One thing I know is that you're ready to STOP living paycheck-to-paycheck.

I am going to share with you everything I did to go from zero dollars in savings to $100k in savings in one year. Whether you're a business owner or an employee, it doesn't matter. I believe you can save one year's living expenses, drown your debt and get control of your financial future.

Rainy days are part of life. It's not *if* they are coming, it's *when* they are coming.

Let's get you ready for the rainy days ahead.

PART 1 –
MONEY MINDSET

"Be not content with littleness...only in magnitude, which is your home...You do not have to strive for it because you already have it. All striving must be directed against littleness."

~ A Course in Miracles

CHAPTER 1

FINANCIAL SELF-SABOTAGE

"Maturity is reached when we realize that no one is going to come rescue us."

~ Marcia Perkins-Reed

Money sabotage comes from an unconscious belief that you are not enough and that you don't deserve abundance.

Your logical mind thinks this is ludicrous. Of course, you want more money and you don't want to be in debt; that's why you're reading this book. Why would you sabotage yourself? That doesn't make sense.

Unfortunately, we were all handed down money messages as children from our caregivers, teachers and society and we are playing those money messages out in our lives, whether we are aware of them or not doesn't matter.

All you need to do is look at your life and your financial situation right now. If you are living in scarcity and deprivation (debt and no savings), you have unhealthy money messages running the show.

Below are some unhealthy money messages you may have received as a child:

- Money doesn't grow on trees

- You have to sacrifice for your family/children

- You have to work hard and struggle to make money

- It's selfish and greedy to want more money

- Live for today, tomorrow is not guaranteed

- There is never enough

- Prince Charming is coming to save you

- Money is the root of all evil

- Money is power

- Money is scarce and hard to get

- Don't let money burn a hole in your pocket

- There are others less fortunate than you

- You're never going to make a lot of money

- It's not spiritual to want money

Many times, we make decisions from our "inner child" and not from our "adult" self. The inner child wants what it wants when they want it – no spending limits, no planned purchases and no savings – spend it all now. That's what children do. Instant gratification is the name of the game.

Self-sabotage is very subtle. We don't even know we're doing it. You can be educated, have multiple degrees, a great job, and still be living in deprivation and lack, because it's not about intelligence, it's about our subconscious and emotional blocks that are holding us back.

The first three chapters of this book are about money mindset; after that we will discuss strategy and tactics. I've learned from coaching hundreds of people over the years that most of the blocks we have around money and success are mental blocks.

See if any of these forms of self-sabotage sound familiar to you:

- Working 12-16 hours a day and never getting ahead

- Working three jobs and never getting ahead

- Workaholism – no life/work balance

- Burnout from overworking

- Repeatedly going into the same line of work even though it is out of alignment with who you are and what you really want

- Putting your needs on hold to take care of others needs

- Bouncing checking or having a negative balance in your bank account

- Running out of money before your next paycheck and having to borrow to cover your bills

- Not balancing your check-book or knowing your financial status

- Saying yes when you want to say no

- Procrastination

- Compulsive spending

- Impulsive buying

- Not doing your due diligence

- Doing the same thing and expecting different results

- Not asking for help

- Hoping someone will save you

- Trying to please everyone

- Settling for crumbs

- Ignoring money matters

- Staying stagnant and not growing

- Surrounding yourself with negative, stagnant people

- Relying on luck, rather than planning

- Ignorance is bliss

- Not maintaining what you have

- Spending more than you make

- Debt, debt, debt

- Keeping secrets about your financial situation

- Living large on the outside, but behind closed doors you are financially drowning

- Hoarding

- Becoming attached to what you have

- Not planning for the future

- Never getting rid of the old to make room for the new

- Borrowing from Peter to pay Paul

I'm sure you can relate to some, or perhaps many, of the ways we self-sabotage ourselves.

In my 20s, I had more than 10 credit cards. As soon as I graduated from college and got a "good" job in the legal field, the credit card companies came calling and I answered enthusiastically. I had every department store credit card under the sun as well as all major credit cards. I also had a car payment. I spent way beyond my means and paid only the minimum payment on my credit cards. I lived like this for years because I felt deprived inside and deep down I didn't believe that I was enough. Spending impulsively and compulsively filled the void temporarily.

What is the void?

That you are not enough. That you aren't worthy to have money in the bank, to live abundantly and prosperously and to enjoy life; to put yourself at the top of the list. To really believe that you matter and your dreams and goals are important. To forgive yourself for the mistakes of your past.

WRITE IT DOWN

I want you to write down the top 10 ways you are self-sabotaging yourself right now. You may not know "why" you are self-sabotaging, but let's start with just acknowledging the ways you are self-sabotaging in your life. Write down your top 10 from the list above.

1. _____

2. _____

3. _____

4. _____

5. _____

6. _____

7. _____

8. _____

9. _____

10. _____

CREATE A CONTRASTING BEHAVIOR

For every self-sabotaging behavior you wrote down, I want you to now write down what the contrasting behavior would be. For example, if one of your self-sabotaging behaviors is "Saying yes when you want to say no," then the contrasting behavior might be instead of saying yes, give yourself 24 hours to think about a request and make a decision only after you've had time to reflect. Don't say yes without a pause."

1. _____

2. _____

3. _____

4. _____

5. _____

6. _____

7. _____

8. _____

9. _____

10. _____

Most of the time, we are operating out of default habits and unfortunately we have a lot of unconscious habits and behaviors.

This chapter is about bringing our self-sabotaging behaviors to the light of day and acknowledging that we are not perfect and it's okay.

We are Flaw-some!

The good news is you picked up this book and that's your soul guiding you to heal your blocks so you can truly live a life of abundance and prosperity.

You must be committed to no longer living paycheck-to-paycheck.

Print out your list of sabotaging and contrasting behaviors and read them every morning and evening. By doing this, you will start noticing when you are "unconsciously" sabotaging yourself. The goal is to catch ourselves before we sabotage ourselves and to start making better choices for ourselves from that place of awareness.

4T Prosperity

Years ago, I was attending Unity church and I signed up for a course called the "4-T Prosperity Workshop." It was a 12-week workshop led by our minister, and I had to sign a contract that I would tithe 10% of all my earnings during that time.

I was scared out of my mind. I was living paycheck-to-paycheck with three young kids to support on my own and could barely make ends meet. How was I ever going to tithe 10% of my income?

Some crazy stuff happened during these 12 weeks:

- I received an unexpected tax refund from a previous tax year that felt like I won the lottery.

- Several years of back child support was finally paid to me.

- I received some help paying my utility bills from a local church organization that my aunt had signed me up for.

You might say it was just a coincidence, but I believe that when fear causes you to hold your hand tight with what little money you do have, the Universe can't put anything into a closed fist.

By tithing, I was opening my hand and not holding so tightly onto the money I had. That created more room to receive more money, and that's exactly what happened.

When we are living in fear, we are actually detracting money from coming into our lives. It's a Catch 22.

How can we not worry when we can't pay our bills?

The answer is FAITH. One of my affirmations during this time was, "God is the source of my supply." Until I took the 4T class, I really believed my paycheck was the only source of my supply. Once I realized I could receive money from other unlimited and unknown sources, money started flowing to me.

Right now you might think that you're stuck because you have limited income and a lot of debt. You're not stuck, only your *thinking* is stuck. If someone told you that you or someone you love were going to die if you didn't figure out how to make more money, save more money and get out of debt in 12 months, I believe you would get creative and resourceful and would be forced to think outside of the box.

When I worked at the law firm, the last year I was earning $48,000 per year, struggling to make ends meet, and living paycheck-to-paycheck. One day, I purchased Barbara Stanny's *Secrets of Six-Figure Woman* and within eighteen months, I was making six figures.

I go into detail about how I left a 17-year in the legal field and created my 6-figure online business in my book, **Quit Your Job and Follow Your Dreams.** Barbara Stanny's book was instrumental because it inspired me to make six figures. I didn't get too attached to the "how," I just focused on my desire to make six figures doing what I loved. That was my affirmation.

What's really crazy is I ended up going from law to making six figures selling hot tubs. I got an outside sales job with no sales experience in a competitive market and started making six figures working only 20-25 hours a week.

It was a miracle to watch this unfold. My fear kept trying to hold me back and I just kept writing my affirmations every day, "I am making six figures doing what I love."

As we will talk about later, I have made six figures for years and am really good at creating money out of thin air, but I never learned to save money. There were times over the years that I did save money, but then I would take that money and make a large purchase – like the million-dollar house I bought in 2007.

I was definitely operating from my subconscious limiting beliefs at the time and sabotaging myself. I learned a lot of lessons about what NOT to do.

Warren Buffet says that when the tide goes out, you see who is naked. I was naked when the housing market crashed.

Abraham Maslow once observed that, "A fear of knowing is a fear of doing."

That's why it's important to know how we are self-sabotaging ourselves and to acknowledge our financial shortfalls because then we can do something about it.

This is the first step towards financial independence. Denial keeps you stuck.

For me, having multiple streams of income allows me to save 50% of what I make. Having two years' worth of living expenses in the bank allows me choose how I want to live and work.

I want the same for you. I'm proud of your for picking up this book and looking for answers. Those who search will find what they are looking for if they are persistent.

In the next chapter, we are going to talk about how to manifest faster by using some manifestation tools.

CHAPTER 2

MANIFESTATION TOOLS

"Every time you don't follow your inner guidance, you feel a loss of energy, a loss of power, a sense of spiritual deadness.

~ Shakti Gawain

Meditation changed my life. You may wonder what meditation has to do with manifestation. I have meditated for over 20 years now, and I'm going to explain how I believe it will help you manifest faster.

When we slow down our minds and pause through meditation, we will be led to a connection with a source of deep wisdom within.

We all have a direct line to God. Meditation is your willingness to speak to and hear God.

When we connect with God through meditation, we connect with our own intuition and we slow down our "monkey minds" enough to hear that voice.

Think of a monkey jumping from one tree to another chasing alluring fruit. When we give our attention to too many things at once, spend our time rushing frantically from one appointment or task to another, we are not present. By chronically jumping from activity to activity and from thought to thought within seconds or minutes, we are operating with fragmented attention and degrading our capacity to remain focused.

So, how do we calm down our monkey mind that is always going, going, going?

Michael Singer, author of *The Untethered Soul* says, "In case you haven't noticed, you have a mental dialogue going on inside your head that never stops. It just keeps going and going. Have you ever wondered why it talks in there? How does it decide what to say and when to say it? How much of what it says turns out to be true? How much of what it says is even important?"

He calls this voice our *inner trouble maker* and we all have that voice inside our heads which narrates the world around us, has problems with just about everything, never shuts up, offers conflicting dialogue, and is emotionally reactive. That voice has frequently given us bad advice and been wrong about many things.

The inner trouble maker is simply a construct that our mind creates to feel more in control. The truth is we don't know what's going to happen next, and that makes us very uncomfortable. So, your mind talks all the time as a protection mechanism, a form of defense to make you feel more secure and to buffer you from life.

Michael Singer says, "If you want to free yourself, you must first become conscious enough to understand your predicament. Then you must commit yourself to the inner work of freedom. You do this as though your life depended on it, because it does. As it is right now, your life is not your own, it belongs to your inner roommate (the inner trouble maker), the psyche. You have to take it back. Stand firm in the seat of the witness and release the hold of the habitual mind has on you. This is your life – reclaim it."

It sounds drastic, but we have two voices inside of ourselves – the observer and the witness. The witness is your center of consciousness.

We can connect with that voice through meditation. The other voice – the observer, or as Michael Singer calls it, our *inner trouble maker* – is not our true self.

We don't have to listen to our inner trouble maker and to that incessant chatter in our minds. We have a much deeper place inside, and we can get to that place through a consistent practice of daily meditation.

The inner troublemaker loves creating drama and repeating trauma and it does so over and over endlessly. It also loves keeping you small and stuck.

When you meditate, you are contemplating the nature of your highest self and you will be led to your authentic and true self.

When I start making bad decisions in my life, I know I have not been meditating consistently. When I miss my meditation practice, then my inner troublemaker takes over and I start making unconscious, self-sabotaging decisions.

It takes practice to start hearing that inner voice, and meditation is a great way to connect. It's more about *being* than *doing*. Sit still for 5-20 minutes and let your thoughts float by while repeating a mantra, focusing on your breath, or simply having no thoughts.

At first, it's hard to still your mind. And, of course, your inner troublemaker will try to convince you that there is no benefit to meditating because the benefits aren't instantaneous. It takes practice and time, but I promise if you consistently meditate for 5-20 minutes per day, you will connect with your deep wisdom, with God, and your life will change significantly.

How Meditation Changed My Life

The first time I meditated 20 years ago, I heard a voice, "If you ever want to be a successful writer, you have to get over your fear of public speaking."

At the time, I left my job in the legal field and I wanted to become a full-time writer. I wanted to write books at home by myself without engaging with other people. As I meditated, the voice persisted ("You need to get over your fear of public speaking if you ever want to be a successful writer") until finally I gave in to the voice and went to a Toastmasters meeting. I hated every minute of that Toastmasters meeting and didn't return for six months. The voice was relentless though, so once again, I gave in and went to another meeting.

I had severe anxiety any time I spoke in front of other people and it was a huge step outside of my comfort zone to go to Toastmasters. It didn't get easier, even after a year, but I just forced myself to continue to go, hoping one day it would work. I became President of that Toastmasters club, and then Area Governor, but inside the anxiety and fear was still out of control.

One day, a friend invited me to Speaking Circles® which was created by Lee Glickstein; where small groups of 8-10 people come together to feel at ease when speaking in public. It was at Speaking Circle, I learned to speak from my heart.

Speaking Circles was completely different than Toastmasters; it is designed to connect with people through the eyes, not rehearsing what to say and receiving only positive feedback and applause from the group.

At my very first Speaking Circle, I broke down crying in front of ten strangers. I never cry or show emotion, especially in public. The deep-seated fears I had that everyone wanted me to fail and that they were judging me harshly melted away in that very loving and supportive group.

I went on to become a certified Speaking Circle® facilitator and I quickly got over my deep seated fear of public speaking.

That one act led me to start teaching workshops, which led me to start a website, to do outside sales, to make six figures, to grow an online business through coaching, speaking and of course, to write books.

I would not be here today if I had not started meditating and then followed my own deep wisdom that led me to the next step on my path.

Morning Pages as a Tool

Another tool I use is *The Morning Pages* created by Julia Cameron, author of *The Artist's Way: A Spiritual Path to Higher Creativity*.

Julia Cameron says that she gets her "marching orders" from God in her morning pages.

Morning pages are three pages of hand-written stream of consciousness writing that you do as soon as you wake up.

Many times, I get marching orders to do things (like get over my fear of public speaking) which make no logical sense to me, but I've learned that there is a deeper wisdom and guidance operating and I've learned to trust and to follow it.

Julia describes the morning pages this way, "The morning pages are the primary tool of creative recovery. As blocked artists, we tend to criticize ourselves mercilessly. Even if we look like functioning artists to the world, we feel we never do enough and what we do isn't right. We are victims of our own internalized perfectionist, a nasty internal and external critic, the Censor, who resides in our left brain and keeps up a consistent stream of subversive remarks that are often disguised as the truth…Logic brain is our Censor, our second thoughts. The Censor is part of our leftover survival brain. Our Censor scans our creative meadow for any dangerous beasties. Any original thought can look pretty dangerous to our Censor."

Meditation will help you disconnect from your Inner Censor and connect to the Creator within.

It is impossible to do meditation and morning pages for any extended amount of time and not come into contact with an unexpected inner power.

Money comes from ideas. If you want to make more money, save more money and pay off your debt, I encourage you to use these tools of meditation and morning pages to connect with your deep wisdom within. As you consistently practice, you will be guided to the next step on your path.

If someone would have told me within 18 months of leaving my legal job, I would be making six figures selling hot tubs, working half the time I would have thought they were crazy.

That outside sales job had a lot of benefits:

- Getting over my fear of talking to people

- It helped me learn to accept rejection

- I learned the art of sales

- I got out of my comfort zones

- I became more open to receive abundance

- I had more money and time freedom

- It gave me lots of time to be with my children as a single parent, to pursue my dream of writing and to enjoy life.

It all happened because I listened to my inner voice and wisdom. It won't always be easy, and many times it isn't. The reason we get stuck financially is because we become stagnant and because we are operating from our lower self (censor/inner troublemaker/habitual self).

Set your intention now that you want to make more money (six figures or higher), get out of debt, and save at least one year's living expenses.

In my book, **Work From Home & Make 6-Figures**, I go over the exact blueprint I used to take my online business from a few thousand per month to $20k+ per month.

Being financially independent is about having power, options, choices and freedom. You aren't a victim. You do have a choice to change your financial life.

In the next chapter, we will talk about the phenomena of being an underearner (someone who earns below what they are capable of earning) and how NOT to be one.

CHAPTER 3

OVERCOMING UNDEREARNING

"There's this nagging little voice, way back in my head – more a feeling than a voice: you shouldn't want money. You shouldn't be telling others to want it either. It's bad, It's wrong. It's like a finger wagging at me, Bad girl. You shouldn't be after money."

~ Barbara Stanny, Secrets of Six Figure Woman

Being an underearner means you have the talent, skills and ability to make more, but you stay stuck in lower-paying jobs. You have a high-tolerance for low pay.

The average median income in the U.S. is about $50k and hasn't changed much in the last few years. My two brothers and I all make six figures and I often wonder why the three of us are all high-income earners.

My brothers both began their careers earning average wages. My youngest brother accepted an offer with a company in a completely different field than the college degree job he had for several years; that enabled him to double his income and started making six figures.

It's hard to change gears, especially when you've done the same thing for a long time. Switching career paths takes courage as well as faith and sometimes your paycheck can increase, and other times you might have to temporarily take a pay cut.

It's important to consider how much joy you have from your job. My joy level for what I do for a living is a 10, and I know my brothers both love what they do.

My father is 83 years old and still works full time as a water meter reader and loves what he does. He's been doing this job, which is his second career, for over 20 years now. His first career was managing a men's retail clothing store, and he did that for over 30 years.

After 30 years, he was burned out and needed a change. I actually found the job listing in the classified ads of a local paper and gave it to him. I thought it would be a great way for him to be outdoors, not be required to wear a suit, and ride around in a truck all day.

20+ years later, he's still doing it and loves it. He doesn't make six figures yet, but he's happy, lives within his means, has a huge savings account, and does not live paycheck-to-paycheck.

My other brother is in the accounting field and was not afraid to change companies to advance his career and make more money. He didn't get too comfortable at any one job.

The common denominator among my two brothers and I is that we seized opportunities and did not remain stagnant.

If you're making less money than you should be at this point in your life, it's probably because you have become way to comfortable and have settled for crumbs.

> "I bargained with Life for a penny,
> And Life would pay no more,
> However I begged at evening
> When I counted my scanty store;
>
> For Life is just an employer,
> He gives you what you ask,
> But once you have set the wages,
> Why, you must bear the task.
>
> I worked for a menial's hire,
> Only to learn, dismayed,
> That any wage I had asked of Life,
> Life would have paid."
>
> — Jessie B. Rittenhouse

The problem isn't that we dream too big, the problem is that we dream too small. We accept far less than we are worth.

DON'T DEVALUE YOUR MAGIC

Years ago when I was working with my amazing business coach, we were putting together my new bestselling author program and he suggested I charge $5000 for a 12-week done-for-you program. I thought he was crazy and said, "No one is going to pay $5000 for this." He said, "They absolutely will. Don't devalue your magic."

He was right and I was wrong.

The first month, I didn't listen to him because I didn't believe people would pay $5000 for what I was doing. So I charged $3000 because I had a lot of fear that I wouldn't get clients at the $5000 price point.

That month, I signed up four new clients. On the weekly coaching call, he said, "Michelle, you just left $8000 on the table ($2000 x 4 new clients). What could you and your family have done with $8000?" Darn! He was right. If I had charged $5000 like he told me to, I would have had an extra $8000 in my bank account that month.

The next month I raised my price to $4000 and, again, I had four people sign up. His comment to me once again was, "Michelle, you just left $4000 on the table ($1000 x 4 new clients). What could you and your family have done with $4000?"

Darn! He was right again. The next month I listened to him and I had my first $22k+ month.

I was undervaluing my services.

Part of it was self-esteem issues, chronic self-sabotage, and the other part was my fear of not getting any clients at the higher price points.

Luckily, my coach advised me, "Don't go broke going elephant hunting." So, I also sold lower-cost training programs to people who could not afford my high-ticket program.

WHERE ARE YOU UNDERVALUING YOURSELF?

Is fear holding you back from making a change in your current career, from asking for a raise, from changing career paths, or from charging your clients more?

Here's some signs that you are an Underearner from Barbara Stanny, in her book, *Overcoming Underearning: A Five-Step Plan to a Richer Life:*

1. I often give away my services (volunteering, or working more hours than I'm actually paid).

2. It's so hard to ask for a raise (or to raise fees) that I just don't do it.

3. I actually dislike money and/or the people who have it.

4. I am proud of my ability to make do with little. There's nobility in being poor.

5. I blame someone or something else for my financial situation (the IRS, my ex-husband).

6. I find ways to avoid dealing with money (bartering, credit cards).

7. I tend to sabotage myself at work (apply for jobs I'm not qualified for or low-paying jobs, stop short of reaching goals, change jobs a lot).

8. I work very, very hard (long hours, several jobs). Or I go into excess then collapse.

9. I fill my free time with endless chores and tasks.

10. I am in debt, with little savings, and no idea where my money is going.

11. I have a family history of debt and/or underearning.

12. I am vague about my earnings (overestimate or underestimate income; see gross, not net).

13. I continually put others' needs before my own.

14. I am frequently in pain or stress about money.

15. Recognition and praise are more important to me than money.

The more of these statements that are true, then you're probably earning less than your potential–despite your desire to make more.

Barbara Stanny says the definition of an Underearner is "One who earns less than her potential despite her need or desire to do otherwise."

8 STEPS TO OVERCOME UNDEREARNING:

Step 1: Identify your #1 negative patterns around money and put it in writing. Examples include: living above your means, compulsive shopping, not saving any money, high credit card debt, giving away your time, undercharging, etc.

Step 2: Make a plan to correct this pattern. Sometimes the problem is an emotional one and you need a good therapist to help you remove those emotional blocks. If it's simply a matter of not focusing and paying attention to your money patterns, then you will work on some of these issues in the upcoming chapters.

Step 3: Write out a money biography. Include things like your job, salary, amount of debt, mistakes you made during that time period. For example, in 2007, I purchased a million-dollar house with my ex-fiancé. We split up that same year and he left me with the million-dollar mortgage. Instead of selling the house that I couldn't afford by myself, I took on 2-3 jobs to pay for everything. I was in way over my head. When we put in writing our mis-steps, it's easier to connect the dots to see how we got to the place we are at now.

Step 4: Make a vow to yourself that you are not going to be an underearner anymore and that you are worth a lot more.

Step 5: Keep your commitments. It's important as you work on your money issues to follow through with what you say you are going to do. No more saying yes when you want to say no. It's important to keep promises to yourself as well.

Step 6: Put yourself first and stop trying to help or enable others when you need to put on your oxygen mask or you will die.

Step 7: Meditate and journal every day so you stay connected to the deep wisdom inside which will direct your next steps on the path to having financial freedom.

Step 8: From the list below, write down any financial red flags and work on fixing them.

Red Flags You Don't Want to Ignore:

- I owe back taxes

- I haven't filed my taxes

- I pay the minimum amount on my credit cards

- I don't have a savings account

- I don't know the total amount of debt I have

- I don't know how much money I have in my bank account

- I let other people handle my finances

- I make late payments on important bills

- I shop compulsively and overspend

- I have poor credit

- Creditors are calling me

- I use credit cards for cash advances

- I am being sued by a creditor and have ignored the paperwork

Circle any of these that apply to you. This is your "troublemaker" list that you are going to start working on. If we ignore the troublemakers, then they will soon turn into financial catastrophes.

Next I want to talk about another reason people are underearners—because they have a subconscious income ceiling.

WHAT IS YOUR INCOME CEILING?

From your money biography above, see what your income ceiling is. What is the most amount of money you have ever earned?

Let's create a new financial goal for you:

"I am making $_____ doing what I love to do in the next 12-18 months."

When I was still making under $50,000 a year at the law firm, I started writing this affirmation dozens of times as part of my morning ritual: *"I am making six figures doing what I love to do,"* and within 18 months, I transitioned to an outside sales job making six figures working half the time.

Don't worry about the *how*, just make the commitment to go above your income ceiling. In my case, I doubled it. I know it's tempting to say, 'I want to make a million dollars,' but let's be real and not live in fantasy land. You're not going to go from making $50,000 (or whatever your current income is) to making $1 million in the next year or so.

I'm 100% certain you can change your financial future. Desire + Awareness + Strategies + Support is the roadmap to get there.

In Chapters One through Three, we have been working on the mental game of money–the mindset. We've acknowledged where we are and where we want to go. Next up, we are going to talk about your "outgoing" expenses and then your "incoming money." These are two areas in which you have full control. You can reduce your living expenses and increase your income. I think it's important to do both.

PART 2 –
MINIMIZE YOUR OUTGOING

"If your outgo exceeds your income,
then your upkeep will be your downfall."

~ Bill Earle

CHAPTER 4

POWER OVER PURCHASES

*"Don't tell me where your priorities are.
Show me where you spend your money and I'll
tell you what they are."*

~ James W. Frick

You might not be able to change your job or income right now, but you absolutely can change your spending habits.

I grew up before the internet, and the only way to make purchases was to physically go to the store and buy things or order from magazines such as Montgomery Wards, Sears, or a specialty magazine.

Now, every product under the sun is at our fingertips, available with one-click of a button which means the temptation to spend, spend, spend is there 24/7.

It's fun buying things; however, it's not fun paying the credit card bill when it comes due.

So why do we overspend?

There are many reasons – we want what we want when we want it and we want instant gratification. I spoke earlier about not letting our inner child run the show and implementing the 24-hour rule before making any purchases over $100.

Now, I want to speak about a deeper reason that many people may have for over-spending – **not having any passion or purpose in their life.**

I believe that when we are working in a job that lacks passion or purpose, we overspend on things we don't need to fill the void.

I wrote an entire book about this subject, *How to Find Your Passion: 23 Questions That Can Change Your Entire Life* and I want to share a story with you from my book:

"On October 23, 1992, I serendipitously met country music singer and actor Billy Ray Cyrus after a concert he performed at and had the pleasure of spending a few hours chatting with him.

10/23/1992, Billy Ray Cyrus and I after a concert at the Patriot Center in Fairfax, VA.

During our time together, Billy Ray asked me:

"What are your dreams?"

At the time, my marriage had recently ended. I was struggling to financially support my three children, living paycheck-to-paycheck in a high-stress job in the legal field, I was having severe panic attacks that led me to the emergency room where I thought I was having a heart attack, and my older brother and best friend, Michael, was diagnosed with AIDS and was dying. I was 29 years old.

Needless to say, it was a dark time in my life and I was living in survival mode. I didn't have the time or energy to think about "dreams."

When you are struggling and in survival mode, you simply don't have the capacity to reflect on higher level things like *dreams*.

Abraham Maslow spoke about this in his hierarchy of needs which are:

- **Basic Needs** – Physiological needs: food, water, warmth, rest

- **Safety Needs** – security, safety

- **Belongingness and Love Needs** – intimate relationships, friends

- **Esteem Needs** – prestige and feelings of accomplishment

- **Self-Actualization** – achieving one's full potential,
  including creative activities

Anyone struggling to get their basic physical and/or psychological needs met is not in a frame of mind to focus on self-actualization.

Billy Ray's question struck a chord deep inside of me. During our conversation, Billy Ray said, "We all have a dream buried inside of us and it's our job to go out and find that dream and once we do, we must never ever give up on our dream."

I took Billy Ray's advice and went out searching for this elusive dream; the one that would bring me a deep feeling of purpose, passion and fulfillment; the things that were severely lacking in my life at the time.

It took about a year of soul-searching before I figured it out. Once again, it was because of a question I read in a tiny book that fell into my hands at the bookstore. That book was *How to Find Your Mission in Life* by Richard Bolles.

When I read the question, I immediately knew the answer and what my dream was. I suddenly felt renewed and alive with purpose, passion and direction in my life.

The life-changing question in Richard Bolles book was "What do you love to do where you lose all sense of time?"

Pause and think about that question for a few moments before reading on.

When I read that question and reflected on it, I suddenly drifted back to my childhood remembering how I loved to write; how five hours of writing seemed like five minutes to me. I loved writing poetry, essays, short stories and even reports for school. Writing is where I lost all sense of time.

Unfortunately, as we "grow up" and become adults, we leave behind our childhood interests and passions and take the more practical path of getting a job that pays the bills. We often choose salaries over our soul's aspirations.

The unfortunate part is that when you're stuck in a job you hate, it can feel like a prison.

I worked in the legal field as a paralegal in a high-stress environment for 17 years until I couldn't breathe any longer. It was literally sucking the life out of me.

Rumi reminds us, "What you are seeking is seeking you."

When Billy Ray Cyrus asked me what my dreams were, it started me down a path that eventually led me to the answer I was looking for."

I talk about this story in all of my books because without that serendipitous meeting with Billy Ray Cyrus, I would not be where I am today. It changed the entire trajectory of my life.

If you're working without passion or purpose, you may be shopping and buying things you don't need to fill a void.

Tama J. Kieves, author of *This Time I Dance: Trusting the Journey of Creating the Work You Love,* was a Harvard lawyer, who left her successful, 6-figure corporate job to follow her dream of writing, says:

"The wrong career creates the need for money. Only the repressed turn reckless. The expressed have better things to do. Live your dreams and you will live in balance."

"Maybe you think that cutting down on material consumption sounds like restraint, deprivation, limitation, a lock and key on your financial liberty. But get ready to undo limits. This path is about real freedom – not just freedom to be rash because you're bored and have cash."

Boredom leads to overspending. Being in the wrong career leads to overspending. Not feeling fulfilled and purposeful leads to overspending.

In my book, I refer to being in the wrong career as having a "bondage job" – one that leaves you feeling drained spiritually, emotionally, mentally and maybe even physically at the end of the day.

My dad told he has a co-worker that comes in every single day to work and says the same thing, "I hate this job and I wish I didn't have to be here."

That's a terrible way to live. I understand we have to pay the bills, but let me offer some clarification about work.

Elizabeth Gilbert, author of the New York Times bestselling books, *Eat Pray Love* and *Big Magic*, wrote a blog post about the four important distinctions between a job, a career, a hobby and a calling and I want to share her post with you because I think it will help you find more clarity. It did for me.

Elizabeth Gilbert's blog post:

"Dear Ones - I get a lot of questions from people who are seeking purpose and meaning in their lives. And I get a lot of questions from people who are seeking career advice – especially about creative careers. And I get a lot of questions from people who are absolutely confused about where their energy is going in life, and why.

For anyone out there who is seeking purpose, meaning and direction in their lives, I thought it might be useful today to define and differentiate four very important words that relate to **HOW WE SPEND OUR TIME IN LIFE.**

Are you ready?

The four very important words are:

1. HOBBY

2. JOB

3. CAREER

4. VOCATION/CALLING

These four words are often interconnected, but they are NOT interchangeable.

Too much of the time, we treat these words like they are synonyms, but they are NOT. They are gloriously distinct and should remain gloriously distinct. Each is wonderful and important in its own way. I think a lot of the pain and confusion that people face when they are trying to chart their lives is that they don't understand the meaning of these words – or the expectations and demands of each word.

So, let me break down what I consider to be the definitions and differences.

1) **HOBBY** – A hobby is something that you do for pleasure, relaxation, distraction, or mild curiosity. A hobby is something that you do in your spare time. *Hobbies can come and go in life* – you might try out a hobby for a while, and then move on to something new. I grew up in a family where everyone had hobbies (my grandmother made rag rugs; my grandfather made jewelry out of old spoons; etc.) and I have hobbies myself. Gardening was my hobby a few years ago; now it's Karaoke and collage-making. You can tell when something is a hobby because your attitude toward it tends to be *relaxed* and *playful*. The stakes are SUPER low with hobbies. Sometimes you might make a bit of money out of your hobby, but that's not the point – nor does it need to be. Hobbies are important because they remind us that not everything in life has to be about productivity and efficiency and profit and destiny. Hobbies are mellow. This is a wonderful reminder, and the concept should relax you. Hobbies prove that we have spare time – that we are not just slaves to the capitalist machine or to our own ambitions. You don't NEED a hobby, mind you, but it's awfully nice to have one. Even the word itself is adorable and non-threatening: HOBBY! What a cute word. Go get one. You have nothing to lose, and it'll probably make you happier. Also, my grandparents would approve. Back before TV, everyone had hobbies. It's nice. No big deal.

2) **JOB** – You may not *need* a hobby, but you do absolutely *need* a job. Unless you have a trust fund, or just won the lottery, or somebody is completely supporting you financially... you need a job. Actually, I would argue that even if you DO have a trust fund or a winning lottery ticket or a generous patron, you should still have a job. I believe there is great dignity and honor to be found in having a job. A job is how you look after yourself in the world. I always had a job, or several jobs, back when I was an unpublished, aspiring writer. Even after I'd already published three books, I still kept a regular job, ***because I never wanted to burden my creativity with the responsibility of paying for my life.*** Artists often resent having jobs, but I never resented it. Having a job always made me feel powerful and secure and free. It was good to know that I could support myself in the world, and that I would never starve, no matter what happened with my creativity. **Now, here's the most essential thing to understand about a job: IT DOESN'T HAVE TO BE AWESOME.** Your job can be boring, it can be a drag, it can even be "beneath you". Jobs don't need to be soul-fulfilling. Really, they don't. I've had all kinds of weird and lame jobs; it doesn't matter, you don't need to love your job; you just need to have a job and do it with respect. Of course, if you absolutely hate your job, by all means look for another one, but try to be philosophical about why you have this job right now. (Some good philosophical reasons for staying in a crappy job right now include: You are taking care of yourself; you are supporting your beloved family; you are saving up for something important; you are paying off debts. The list of reasons to have a job – even a bad job – goes on and on, and honor abides within all those reasons.) Don't judge yourself about your job and

never be a snob about anyone else's job. We live in a material world and everyone has to do something for money, so just do whatever you have to do, collect your paycheck, and then go live the rest of your life however you want. Your job does not need to be how you define yourself; you can create your own definitions of your purpose and your meaning, pulled from deep within your imagination. A job is vital, but don't make it YOUR LIFE. It's not that big a deal. It's just a job – a very important and also not-at-all important thing.

3) **CAREER** – A career is different from a job. A job is just a *task* that you do for money, but a career is something that you **build over the years with energy, passion, and commitment**. You don't need to love your job, but I hope to heaven that you love your career – or else you're in the wrong career, and it would be better for you to quit that career and just go find yourself a job, or a different career. Careers are best done with excitement. Careers are huge investments. Careers require ambition, strategy, and hustle. Your career is a relationship with the world. I used to have jobs, but now I have a career. My career is: AUTHOR. That means: Professional Writer. When I think about my work in terms of my career, I need to make sure that I'm building good relationships in the publishing world, and making smart decisions, and managing myself well within a realm that is more public than private. I need to pay attention to what critics are saying about my work, and how my books are selling, and how well I'm meeting my deadlines. I need to tend to my career with respect and regard, or else I will lose it. I need to honor my contracts and my contacts. When I make decisions about my life, I need to think about whether this would be good or bad for

my career. If I win an award, that's good for my career. If I get caught in a hotel room with a pile of cocaine and six exotic dancers, that's bad for my career. (Actually, now that I think about it, maybe that would be AWESOME for my career! Gotta look into that! HA!) Let me make something very clear about careers: **A career is a good thing to have if you really want one, but YOU DO NOT NEED TO HAVE A CAREER.** There is absolutely nothing wrong with going through your entire life having jobs, and enjoying your hobbies, and pursuing your vocation, but never having "a career". A career is not for everyone. A career is a choice. But if you do make that choice, make sure that you really care about your career. Otherwise, it's just an exhausting marathon, for no reason. I really care about my career, but it's not the most important thing in my life. Not even close. The most important thing in my life is my....

4) **VOCATION** – The word "vocation" comes to us from the Latin verb "vocare" – meaning "*to call*". *YOUR VOCATION IS YOUR CALLING*. Your vocation is a summons that comes directly from the universe and is communicated through the *YEARNINGS OF YOUR SOUL*. While your career is about a relationship between you and the world; your vocation is about the relationship between you and God. Vocation is a private vow. Your career is dependent upon other people, but your vocation belongs only to you. You can get fired from your career, but you can never get fired from your vocation. Writing was my vocation long before I was lucky enough to get the career of an "Author" – and writing will always be my vocation, whether my career as an Author keeps working out or not. This is why I can approach my career with a certain sense of calm –

because I know that, while I obviously care about career, I am not defined by it. When I consider my writing in terms of my career, I have to care what the world thinks about me. But when I consider my writing in terms of my vocation, **I TRULY DO NOT GIVE A FUCK WHAT THE WORLD THINKS ABOUT ME.** My career is dependent upon others; my vocation is entirely my own. The entire publishing world could vanish, and books could become obsolete, and I would still be a writer − because that's my vocation. That's my deal with God. *You do not need to make money from your vocation in order for it to have meaning.* Writing had meaning for me LONG before you ever heard of me, and long before anyone else wanted me to do it.

Vocation has nothing to do with money, with career, with status, with ambition. I often see people corrode their vocation by insisting that it become a career − and then making career decisions that destroy their vocation. (Amy Winehouse's career destroyed her vocation, for instance.) The day that I feel my career is destroying my vocation, I will quit my career and go get a job, so that I can protect my vocation. But I will never quit my vocation. Nobody even needs to know about your vocation, in order for it to have meaning. Your vocation is holy because it has nothing to do with anyone else. *Your vocation can be anything that brings you to life and makes you feel like your soul is animated by purpose.* Tending to your marriage can be your vocation. Raising your children can be your vocation. Teaching people how to take care of their health can be your vocation. Visiting your elderly neighbors can be your vocation. I have a friend who finds his vocation in picking up garbage off the streets wherever he goes; this is his gesture of love toward his fellow man. Searching for light and peace and meaning can be your vocation.

Forgiveness can be your vocation. Brother Lawrence was a 17th century monk who worked his whole life washing dishes in a monastery (because washing dishes was his JOB) but his vocation was to see God in everything and everyone, and that is why he radiated grace. (Awesome vocation, by the way. People came from all over the world to watch Brother Lawrence wash dishes, because of the way he radiated divine love in every act. THAT'S vocation.) I admire the Roman Catholic Church for understanding the sanctity of vocation, and for teaching that the purest human vocation is LOVE. A vocation is the highest expression of your human purpose, and therefore you must approach it with deepest reverence. You can be called to your vocation by what you love (for instance: I love writing), or you can be called to your vocation by what you hate (for instance: I know people who dedicate themselves to social justice because of their hatred for violence and inequality.) If you don't have a vocation and you long for one, you can pray for one. You can ask the universe with humility to lead you to your vocation – but then you must pay VERY close attention to the clues and signs that point you toward your vocation. **Don't just pray and WAIT. Instead, pray and SEEK**. Everyone wants the lightning strike, but the path to your vocation is usually a trail of bread crumbs, instead. Look for clues. No clue is too small; no vocation is insignificant. Don't be proud; be attentive. **What brings your soul to life**? What makes you feel like you are not just a meat puppet – not just here to work hard and pay bills and wait to die? You cannot be lazy or entitled about your vocation, or apathetic, or fatalistic, or calculating. You cannot give up on it, if things don't "work out" – whatever that even means. You must work closely with your intuition in order to find your highest meaning in life. This is hard work sometimes, but it is divine work, and it is always worth it.

(Here's a possibility, for instance: Searching for your vocation can be your vocation!) You can choose your hobbies, your jobs, or your careers, but you cannot choose your vocation; you can only accept the invitation that has been offered to you or decline it. You can honor your vocation, or you can neglect it. You can worship it, or you can ignore it. A vocation is offered to you as a sacred gift, and it is yours to care for, or to lose. When you treat your vocation as sacred, you will see your whole life as sacred − and everyone else's lives, too. When you are careless about your vocation, you will treat your whole life carelessly − and other people's lives, too. Your vocation will become clear to you through the act of **PAYING ATTENTION** to your senses and your soul, and to what in the world causes you to feel love or hate. You will be led to your vocation, though the path is not always obvious. You must participate in its unfolding. Do not fall asleep on this job. Your vocation is **hinted** at through your talents, tastes, passions, and curiosities. Your vocation is calling you, even when you can't quite hear it. (*"What you are seeking is seeking you" − Rumi*.) When you embrace a vocation, and commit yourself to that vocation, your mind becomes a quieter place. When you accept the divine invitation of your vocation, you will become strong. You will know that − as long as you are tending to your vocation − everything will be fine.

My feeling is that people look for purpose in life without understanding these four words: HOBBY, JOB, CAREER, VOCATION. People blend these four concepts, or mistake them, confuse them, or try to have all four at once, or pretend that they are all the same thing. Or people just generally get freaked out and confused, because they haven't thought these words through, or decided which ones are most important.

(Or which ones are most important RIGHT NOW.) People generally want to know, "*What am I doing with my life?*", but they don't slow down long enough to really think about these four different aspects of this question – the four different possibilities for where our time and energy goes. People worry so much about their careers, for instance, that they often forget to pay attention to their vocations. Or people get so seduced by the grandeur of their vocations that they forget to have a job, and so they stop taking care of themselves and their families in the material world...which will only bring suffering. (Remember: Even Brother Lawrence had a job. He was not too proud to wash dishes.) Or people are so busy chasing social status and personal advancement that they forget to make time for the relaxing joy of having a sweet little hobby. And oftentimes people mistake a sweet little hobby for something that they think should be a job, or a career, or a vocation. **Don't try to blend what perhaps doesn't need to be blended. Don't mistake a job for a career, or a career for a vocation, or a vocation for a hobby, or a hobby for a job. Be clear about what each one is and be clear about what can be reasonably expected from each one and be clear about what is demanded of you with each one.**

Here's another thing I see happening: people get so embarrassed or resentful about their lousy day jobs that they forget to be grateful that they have a job at all – and this causes only more anxiety and confusion, which again, will make them stop paying reverent attention to their vocation, or enjoying their hobbies, or making plans for a career.

We live in a real world that is heavy sometimes with real-life obligations, but we also have souls that deserve care and attention. We can pay attention to our worldly ambitions and pleasures (hobbies, jobs, careers) without neglecting our mystical, otherworldly, beautiful and often impractical vocations. We can pay attention to all of it – but this requires sitting still at times and really thinking things through, with courage and dignity. And it requires an understanding of terms.

The important thing is to be sober and careful and attentive enough to know what you are REALLY talking about when you consider the question, *"What am I doing with my life?"*

It isn't easy to answer this question but understanding and respecting these four different words might be a start.

And when in doubt, at least *try* SOMETHING. As the wonderful poet David Whyte says: "*A wrong-headed but determined direction is better than none at all.*"

Good luck out there, brave seekers!

Onward,
LG

****

When I read that post years ago, a light bulb went off and it helped me to understand my past and see which paychecks were from "jobs," which ones were from a career, and which ones were hobbies, and what my calling was.

Writing books is a *calling* I have had for a long time. Working for 17 years as a paralegal was a career I enjoyed for the majority of those years, until I got burned out and it began to drain the life out of me. I've also had hobbies that I tried to turn into "jobbies" that didn't work out.

Think about your jobs and/or businesses you've had over your lifetime and apply these four distinctions.

Even if you've enjoyed a job for twenty years, it doesn't mean you have to stay there for your entire life if you've lost your passion for it. That would be like staying in a loveless or passionless marriage.

It's important to reclaim your power over your purchases because that is the path to financial freedom. First, however, we need to understand why we shop and why we overspend. Not having a purpose or passion at work can be the cause of overspending for many people.

If you really love your job and have a passion for it, but have a problem with overspending and going into debt, then it's time to work on your overspending so you can work up to saving 50% of what you make.

Here are six tips to reclaim power over your purchases:

1. Implement a 24-hour rule for purchasing anything over $100. You must go home and wait 24 hours and then decide if you really wanted that "thing." Often, I find that I was being impulsive. I've saved hundreds and probably thousands of dollars by having this rule. This rule helps me a lot.

2. Start saving your receipts and create small baskets or file folders with categories such as clothing, eating out, groceries, gifts, household decorations, books, _____ (your weakness item that you overspend on – could be shoes, watches, or jewelry). Then, review your spending habits every 30 days. The goal is to bring awareness

to your unconscious spending and see where you can take some of this money and put it into your savings account which you'll be starting soon.

3. Cut up or freeze your credit cards and stop creating more debt.

4. My daughter signed up for a program called Consumer Alliance and it has saved her over $14,000 in interest she would have been paying to the credit card companies had she made the minimum payments (which she was doing). I don't know all the details about the program, but the core of it is that they negotiate your interest rate down with the credit card company, saving you hundreds and maybe thousands of dollars, and then you make the payment to them with a fixed term for payoff. You can never use that credit card again. My daughter's debt will be paid off in two years instead of NEVER!

5. Write a summary of all of your monthly bills and adjust your expenses according to these guidelines:

Giving	10%
Saving	10%
Food	10-15%
Utilities	5-10%
Housing	25%
Transportation	10%
Health	5-10%
Insurance	10-25%
Recreation	5-10%
Personal Spending	5-10%
Miscellaneous	5-10%

6. Get rid of any expenses or items you have purchased to keep up with the Joneses. The Joneses are broke, have debt up to their eyeballs, and are in foreclosure! You can sell your items on Craigslist, eBay, Facebook Marketplace or put up a post on your social media. If it's a car with a high payment, then trade it in for a car that you can afford that is only 10% of your income.

Chris Hogan, author of the book *The Everyday Millionaire*, says, "If you live fake rich now, you'll retire real broke later."

DEBT IS A THREAT TO YOUR DREAMS

Debt is the #1 threat to saving money, having more choices and being financially free. It actually hijacks your future and keeps you trapped in situations you might not want to be in. When you have debt, you pay interest and instead of your money working for you, you are allowing someone else to use your money for their own benefit.

The goal of this book is for you to pay off all of your debt, save one year of living expenses in a savings account, and create a brand new financial future for you and your family.

TO RENT OR TO OWN

I've been listening to a lot of successful people and experts; many of them are recommending that you not go in debt for a house and instead rent within your means.

There was also a study done that the happiest people are people who rent.

I guess because I've owned a few houses, including a million-dollar house that went to a short sale, I am hesitant to take on all that debt. The reality is if I buy a home for $400k, which is the average price in my area, I'm going to end up paying $800k for that house with interest and I'm not willing to take on that amount of debt.

I've been renting a beautiful 2300 square foot rancher on the water for 4+ years and the rent payment is less than 25% of my income. Since it's not my house, I have no unexpected expenses and I don't spend money on endless home improvements.

Some well-meaning people remind me about tax deductions from owning a house, but the taxes for a house in my area are outrageous and would probably offset any savings I would get from a tax write-off. Plus, I believe that most houses are money pits;. except for new construction. If I could get an affordable, new construction home in my area, I would consider it, but the prices are too high for me to settle for something I don't want.

You have to make this decision for yourself, but if you're house-poor you might want to consider selling your house and renting. The woman I rent my house from is 107 years old and says she has no desire to sell it because she might want to move back one day! ☺

I feel very comfortable here, and I'm taking great care of her house. Her husband built this house 40 years ago and the rental income is nice for her to use for living expenses.

I'm not telling you to do what I'm doing, I'm just sharing my story in case you're conflicted about this. The problem is many people will try to talk you out of it.

If you want to rent instead of own and it makes financial sense, then do that. If you want to own instead of rent and it makes financial sense, then do that.

My new plan is to save $100k a year for five years and to pay cash for a house down the road with no mortgage. I'll write a book about that when it happens!

In the next chapter, we are going to talk about needs vs. wants; something most of us have a skewed perspective on.

—

NEEDS VS. WANTS

"Rich people have a lot of money and spend a little, while poor people have a little money and spend a lot."

~ T. Harv Eker, author of
Secrets of the Millionaire Mind

I listen to a lot of Gary Vaynerchuk videos. If you don't know who Gary V. is, Google him. I love this guy! He took his parent's company, the Wine Library, from $3 million a year to $45 million a year. He's very direct, to the point, and rough around the edges, but he speaks the truth in my opinion.

In one of his recent videos, Gary spoke about being an immigrant and why so many immigrants who come to this country end up having great success by owning businesses. The reason he says is because "They don't buy stupid shit for 15 years" and they work hard.

Gary says when he was in his 20's, he didn't buy stupid sh*t, he was living, eating, and breathing his family business.

I can imagine how hard that is for a kid in his 20's to ignore peer pressure from friends who may not understand his level of work ethic and commitment.

And to have the wherewithal not to try to keep up with the Joneses or to impress his friends. Even when the company was mega successful, Gary V. decided to get a cheaper place to live so he could save more money. He moved from his $2000 a month apartment and leased another one for $1400 a month and put that $600 into savings each month.

I fell into the consumerism trap when I bought my million-dollar house and then spent $35,000 furnishing it and my ex-fiancé spent another $45,000 on just the audio equipment. We even contemplated having our own server and a mirror in the living room that doubled as a television screen.

Excuse my language – but "dumb sh*t!"

Most of us have lost sight of the difference between needs vs. wants.

We live in a celebrity-driven society and we see the mega success of celebrities and we want what they have. I get it. I love nice things, but not at the expense of my freedom.

I wanted to do a chapter on the difference between needs vs. wants because you might be thinking, "I need my BMW" or "I need my designer handbag" or "I need my Rolex."

You don't *need* any of those things. You *want* those things and it's time to look underneath to find out *why* you want those things.

All the time, I see people purchasing designer handbags and clothing when they absolutely cannot afford it.

Look at the chart below by Bankrate.com showing how much people have saved for "emergency savings:"

How much do Americans have in emergency savings?

Enough to cover ...

6+ months	29%
3 to 5 months	18%
Fewer than 3 months	22%
None	23%

Note: 8% responded "don't know/refused."
Source: Bankrate's Financial Security Index, June 6-10, 2018

Bankrate

23% of people have zero saved for an emergency. 22% have fewer than three months! Those aren't good numbers. I want you to be in the 29% percent category having saved at least six months' salary in an emergency savings account and ideally, 12 months.

I'm not at retirement age and I have my own business, so it's really important for me to have backup cash in case something unexpected happens—and guess what? Something unexpected always happens. Don't live in fantasy land, and don't put the burden on others to help you when the unexpected happens because it will happen.

Now, let's define what a need is:

A need is something you *need* to survive like shelter, food, heat, electricity, the basic necessities.

A *want* is something you can survive without.

You may want a million-dollar house on the water, but you actually only need a 2-bedroom apartment, condo, house, or townhouse .

You may want a designer handbag that costs $1200, but you actually only need a $30 handbag to hold all of your stuff.

You may want a Rolex watch, but you only need a $35 watch, or you can just use your smartphone to tell time.

You may want a BMW or a Tesla, but you only need a reliable car that gets you from point A to point B and that can be purchased new for $15 to 20k or used for $10k or less. At the time of this writing, a brand new Tesla costs $35k to $124k. A brand new BMW costs $35k to $147k.

Do you see the difference between wants vs. needs? The lines are blurry, and if your life depended on you saving 12 months of living expenses, you would get crystal clear on the difference between needs vs. wants.

Let's do an exercise.

Write down everything in your life that is a NEED:

1. _____

2. _____

3. _____

4. _____

5. _____

6. _____

7. _____

8. _____

9. _____

10. _____

Now, write down everything in your life that is a WANT:

1. _____

2. _____

3. _____

4. _____

5. _____

6. _____

7. _____

8. _____

9. _____

10. _____

I'm not trying to get you to live like a pauper or completely deprive you off all of your "wants," but I would like you to see the trade-off. Especially if you are buying things on credit. The more you have to "pay," then the less time you have to "play." And the more wants you have, the less savings you will have.

Sometimes we have to go without in order to achieve our goals. If your goal is truly to have financial peace of mind and freedom, then you must start living way below your income, ideally 50%, but if you could get to the point where you have a 25% buffer, that would be amazing.

In his book, *Profit First: Transform Your Business from a Cash-Eating Monster to a Money-Making Machine*, by Mike Michalowicz, he says, "Treating profit like an afterthought, secondary to growth, usually has the effect of running your business into the ground."

Think of your life as a business – the goal of a business is to make a profit and to have sustained profitability.

Right now, you are probably running a cash-challenged and debt-heavy business. It's time to change that.

8 out of 10 businesses fail, and according to a Babson College report, "A lack of profitability is consistently the major reason cited for business discontinuation."

It's the difference between barely surviving and thriving.

After his own failed business and losing millions, Mike came up with the following formula:

"Sales – Expenses = Profit. The solution is profoundly simple: Take your profit first."

It's time for you to be profitable and to treat your financial life like a business.

Mike's book, which I highly recommend, goes into great detail about the "Profit-First Methodology" which is brilliant and has saved a lot of failing businesses.

Your new formula for "YOU, INC." is:

Income – Expenses = Profit.

Get it?

In Section 3, we are going to talk about increasing your income, but first your assignment is to decrease your living expenses so you have a 25% buffer (ideally a 50% buffer).

Look at all of your expenses and see what you can cut, refinance, or restructure. The checklist in Chapter 11 will help you know what action steps to take.

In the next chapter, we are going to talk about how to dump your debt and also how to play the credit game.

CHAPTER 6

LOW DEBT AND HIGH CREDIT SCORES

"We buy things we don't need with money we don't have to impress people we don't like."

~ Dave Ramsey

Debt is dumb. We pay credit card companies on average 21% interest, and with a savings account, the bank pays us an average of 0.09% interest.

And if you buy a $300,000 house at 4.5% interest on a 30-year mortgage, you end up paying $704,000! That's more than double!

Why do we do this?

Because we want things now.

Did you know there are countries that don't have mortgages? Take for example, Sri Lanka. They buy land and over time, the family builds a home on that land, everyone helping with different aspects of the house.

In Canada, the maximum mortgage term is 10 years and most people do a five-year loan.

Let's start by making a plan to reduce your credit card debt. As long as you have reduced your living expenses by 25% you should have more money to pay on your credit cards.

So, how do you pay off your credit card debt and which credit card do you pay off first?

There are two schools of thought:

1. Pay off the highest interest rate credit card

2. Pay off the card with the lowest balance

Most people want to pay off the card with the lowest balance, because it makes them feel good to have one less bill to pay, however, you will be paying more on interest if you do that.

Either way, paying off debt is good. If it makes you feel better paying off the lowest balance card first and then using that money towards paying off the next card, then by all means do that.

Financial guru, Dave Ramsey, advocates paying off small debts first and calls this the "debt-snowball method" which helps you scale your debt mountain.

I personally like feeling I've accomplished something by having fewer accounts to pay, so when I had many credit cards, I paid of the lowest balance first.

Select your preferred method to pay off your credit cards and fill in the chart below:

Credit Card	Balance	Interest Rate	Min. Pymt

I read that the average American carries $38,000 of debt not including mortgages, which is pretty high.

If you have a car payment, it should be no more than 10% of your net income. If you have a high-interest auto loan, a high payment or a luxury car, you should consider selling it and purchasing something more affordable; especially if you have a high debt mountain to climb.

If your credit is good, you can also play the 0% "transfer" game and transfer your higher interest rate card to a zero percent card and then pay that off card in the allotted time.

This can save you hundreds, if not, thousands of dollars on interest.

Speaking of credit, let's talk about how to improve your credit score.

I am not a credit counselor and I have no degrees or certifications in this area, however, I did raise my credit score from 535 to over 800 with three different credit reporting agencies. So, I want to share with you what I did so you can learn from me.

For a couple of years after I had to sell my million dollar house at a short sale, I paid cash for everything. I was afraid to get another credit card because I didn't trust myself and didn't want to end up with a lot of debt once again.

But when I needed to move and buy a car, I had to ask family members to co-sign and I didn't like that. I finally decided to suck it up and play the credit card game.

I applied for my first credit card through Capital One and was approved for an account with a $250 limit. Every month, I would charge $100-$200 on the card and then pay half of the balance. I tried to keep the ratio of available credit to the balance owed at about 30%.

Next, my father added me on as a user to a Bank of America credit card he had. My father charges all of his bills (about $2500+) on his card and then pays it off in full each month. He added me as a user, gave me the extra card and I began doing the same. I would charge business expenses on that card, and then pay it off in full.

This helped my credit tremendously. So, if you have a family member that is willing to do this, eat humble pie and ask them to help you. And if they do agree, never ever be late with that payment.

My credit score began increasing consistently every month. About a year later, I applied for another credit card and was given a $1000 limit. I began using that card and paying half of the balance and keeping credit usage at 30%.

The banks increased my credit limits after I continued making my payments on time each month.

Finally, when my credit score was over 700, I leased a car. I would not recommend leasing a car for most people, however, my son works at Lexus and they had a family and friends deal where they basically gave you an $8000 down-payment and then a low monthly payment equivalent to that of a Hyundai for a brand new Lexus. I took the deal and because I work from home and don't drive to an office daily so I knew I would not be using a lot of mileage; it has worked out perfectly for me.

At the end of the lease term, I'll be able to purchase the car for $18k, and I'm happy with that since it is a $44k car.

Remember, I didn't have any debt when I did this so it worked for me.

I kept playing the credit game and after a couple of years, I applied for a credit card and to my surprise, I was given a $25,000 credit limit! I was shocked!

I had all this credit available and didn't need it, but I used the credit cards and made the payments every month to keep increasing my credit scores.

Right now, all of my scores are in the 800's and everyone is offering me credit.

How come when you don't need credit, they give it to you and when you do need it, they reject you?

Anyway, this is the world we live in. We have to keep our credit scores in good standing because we never know when we will have to move, purchase a vehicle, or have an unexpected emergency come up.

I was able to use the $25,000 credit card I had to put a deposit on a very expensive AirBNB that I was renting in Florida for a business event – my Ocean Writing retreat. I put a $3,000 deposit down using that credit card. I kept most of that balance on the card for about three months, made the minimum payments, but I ended up cancelling the event and getting a full refund. I wasn't strategically doing this to boost my credit, however, it did end up somehow improving my credit score. I cancelled the event because there weren't enough registrations, and it positively affected my credit score just by having that balance on there for three months and making the minimum payments.

If you do the numbers, the credit card had a balance of $3000 and the credit limit was $25,000, I kept that balance on there for three credit cycles and paid interest on it, but it was only 12% usage. I think it helped me because in the eyes of the credit Gods, I paid off that balance in 90 days.

Here are some things that can really hurt your credit score:

- Keeping a high balance to credit limit. You should strive for less than 30% of the credit limit as the highest balance.

- A lot of inquiries in a short amount of time. Don't go crazy and apply for ten credit cards at once. I think I applied for a credit card once a year.

- Never miss a payment; schedule automatic minimum payments on all your credit cards.

- Again, never max out a credit card.

- Collections. Don't ignore that $50 medical bill because it can really do damage to your credit score. Even if it is in error, sometimes you just have to suck it up and pay it so it doesn't affect your credit score. Also, utility companies can report to the credit bureaus so keep that in mind.

- Bankruptcy. You'll take a hit for seven years on that.

- Foreclosure. Short Sale. I went from having a 740 credit score to dropping to 535 when I did my short sale.

- Deed in lieu of foreclosure.

- Not having any credit. Even if you have a secured credit card (make sure they report to the credit bureaus), you need to have credit history.

- Being an authorized user on someone's "bad" account. If you do become a user on someone's credit account, you must be 100% certain they will always pay and pay on time or it will hurt you in the long run.

- Credit report errors. Always get your credit reports once a year and check for accuracy. I had a lot of things removed when I started this process.

- Refinancing your home or taking out a home equity line of credit can negatively affect your credit score.

So, that's what I did to increase my credit score almost 300 points. It didn't happen overnight, but I was able to get my score up and I wish I would have focused on it sooner, rather than later.

I'm not sure about these "credit repair" companies as I have no personal experience with them. However, do your research and ask around. Maybe there is a good one out there that can help you.

You deserve to have good credit. It takes work and time and there are no shortcuts.

In the next chapter, we're going to talk about how to become a Money Magician!

PART 3 –
MAXIMIZE YOUR INCOMING

"The more you learn, the more you earn.

~ Warren Buffett

CHAPTER 7

BECOME A MONEY MAGICIAN

"When your desires are strong enough, you will appear to possess superhuman powers to achieve."

~ Napoleon Hill, Think & Grow Rich

How would you like to be a money magician and have the ability to create money any time you want?

Years ago, I took a money quiz based on eight different archetypes and mine came up as "Money Magician."

Take the money type quiz here: https://moneycoachinginstitute.com/money-type-quiz/

I attribute being a money magician to learning the art of sales.

Sales is the lifeblood and oxygen of any company. Without sales, the company fails. If you want to become a money magician, you must be able to sell.

After 17 years in the legal field, I transitioned to an outside sales job and I tried to quit that job several times in the first year. Luckily, I had a boss who would not let me quit. I remember one conversation that went like this:

"Bob, you don't understand, I'm a single mom with three young kids to support and I can't go weeks without a paycheck."

"Michelle, you're doing great. There is a one-year learning curve and I promise if you stick it out, you'll be making six figures in no time."

Then, magically, the very next day, my sales manager Bob would cherry pick a lead for me and I'd make thousands of dollars in commissions.

I was selling hot tubs and swim spas, in home, in an all-commission job during the real estate boom. People were using their home equity to buy luxury items like hot tubs; I was in the right place at the right time.

I had that job for about 10 years until the real estate market crashed and people quit buying hot tubs so the company filed bankruptcy and laid off their entire sales staff.

If that company had been smart during the growth years, it would have saved money so it could ride out the lean years; instead, the company went under due to a cash flow problem.

I'm telling you this story for a couple of reasons – one, you must learn to sell because if you have that ability and skill, you'll never be broke. And, two, cash flow is king and queen!

Many people, especially introverts like me, hate sales, but I've learned from years of being in sales that sales is really just about developing relationships, deep listening and helping people solve problems.

Gary Vaynerchuk, author of bestselling books like *Crushing It: How Great Entrepreneurs Build Their Business and Influence – And How You Can Too*, says that sales is the foundation of any business and any entrepreneur.

Since I learned the art of sales, I have been making six figures consistently every year. Before I learned sales, I was broke and living paycheck-to-paycheck.

Robert Kiyosaki, author of *Rich Dad, Poor Dad*, is famous for his four quadrants which are:

- Employee – you have a job

- Self-Employed – you own a job

- Business Owner – you own a system that works for you

- Investor – money works for you

I have experience in all four quadrants. The "employee" quadrant has the least flexibility and ability to make more money (unless it's in high ticket sales).

My son works for Lexus; he's 33 years old and makes over $150k per year because he learned how to sell. He started as a server working in restaurants in his teen years. Then, he became a shoe salesman in the ladies shoe department at

Nordstrom's. Next he worked at 24-Hour Fitness in sales, and then he landed the best job yet, selling for Lexus.

I am a huge fan of Lexus. When I was in outside sales for ten years driving 30,000 miles a year, I began having back issues. One day, I went to a car show at the DC convention center and sat in all the cars to see which had the best back support and decided I buy that car. I ended up buying a Lexus and I loved it.

I became friends with the manager of the Lexus, and he was an amazing, top-notch sales guy. He sold me two more Lexus's over a period of time. When I would go in to visit, he would try to hire me to sell at Lexus. He was very persistent. I told him, "I'm a lazy sales person. I make six figures from home working 20-25 hours per week and I have no interest working 50-60 hours per week at Lexus. But I have someone better than me who would love to work here – my son!"

The timing was perfect as my son had just been laid off at one of his jobs, and I set up the interview. He's been there for six years now! There were a lot of growing pains for both him and his manager at Lexus. They are very militant in that dealership and my son needed the Lexus boot-camp that they put him through.

He is now one of their top salesmen and has won numerous awards. He's even been offered a management position which he declined. I don't blame him – managing people requires a special skill and I don't think he would be happy doing that.

So, although he is an "employee" and has a job, he makes six figures, has health insurance, benefits and loves his job.

He's tried a few entrepreneurial things, but he prefers the structure of a sales organization.

When I was selling hot tubs, I was an employee and had health benefits, however, it was 100% commission and if I didn't sell, I didn't make any money.

I am thankful for that job and being able to learn from some of the best managers ever on how to sell. I was horrible in the beginning. In fact, I remember one of my very first appointments, I was so nervous. I was literally, reading from the script in my book and I looked up and the older gentlemen, who I was talking to, fell asleep and was snoring! I was boring him because I wasn't connecting with him. I was reading a script.

Fast forward eighteen months and I was in the top 10% of the company making six figures. That happened for a few reasons:

- I committed to being a top sales person
- I avoided the bottom sales people who complained all the time
- I was mentored by the top sales people
- I had amazing managers who molded and shaped me into a top sales person
- I didn't quit

It was not an easy path because I am an introvert and I had to meet strangers, bond with them in a two-and-a-half-hour appointment and sell a high-ticket product in a one-call close. It's not easy to tell people that the sale is today or never.

Learning the art of sales is paramount to your success and highly beneficial because you will always be able to make money. If you avoid sales, you will probably stay broke.

Some of the best sales people I know were door-to-door sales people. Maybe you have a bad taste in your mouth because you've had a poor experience with an aggressive or obnoxious sales person.

I get it. I've experienced those guys and gals too and it's sad, but it's time to get over it. Commit to not being like them and being a relationship builder, a deep listener and a problem solver instead.

People are always asking Gary V. how they can make money and I've heard him say "Go sell shit." He will tell people to go to the dollar store, buy some in-demand items and then resell them on eBay or Amazon.

If you want to stay stuck, then don't learn how to sell, but if you want to grow and change your financial future, master the art of sales.

This isn't a book to teach you how to sell, however, I'll recommend a few books for you at the end of this chapter, but the best teacher is experience. Even if you have a full time job, get a part time job selling something or start selling stuff on your own.

When I was a kid, I sold a lot of things:

- Lemonade

- Plants

- Girl Scout Cookies

- Tickets to a Neighborhood Skit I created

- Baked Goods for bake sales

- Babysitting Services

- Cleaning Services

I think I was born an entrepreneur. That's why at the end of my 17-year career, I was so miserable because I didn't have any freedom and the only way I could make more money was to trade more of my time. As a single mom, I couldn't do that because I was already leveraged to the max.

Once I was out of the legal field, I learned sales and went on to create multiple streams of income, which is what the next chapter is all about.

RECOMMENDED BOOKS ON SALES:

- *Little Red Book of* Selling by Jeffrey Gitomer

- *Building a Story Brand* by Donald Miller

- *Sell or Be Sold* by Grant Cardone

- *The Greatest Salesman in the World* by Og Mandino

*These are all books I have read and love.

CHAPTER 8

MULTIPLE STREAMS OF INCOME

"Above all I learned that it's entirely possible for any one of us, with average intelligence, to increase our income without selling our soul."

~ Barbara Stanny, author of
Secrets of Six-Figure Women

It was scary when I got the pink slip at the law firm because I was living paycheck-to-paycheck and had no rainy day back-up money. Luckily, they gave me a small severance check and that held me over for a while.

I vowed never to depend on one income stream again and decided I would create multiple streams of income; this way, if one stream dried up, I would have others flowing in.

I still do this today.

Some of the streams of income I created when I left the legal field were:

- Income from my sales job (my main stream of income)

- I became a freelance reporter for the local newspaper

- I taught classes at the local community college as a freelancer

- I started my first website becomea6figurewoman.com in 2005 and created online courses making $1k-$3k part-time

- I studied copywriting and became a paid copywriter bringing in $1000 to $5000 per month

- In 2011, I learned how to create and build WordPress websites and became a freelance web designer which brought in about $2000 to $6000 per month

- In 2013, I created the bestselling author program and that became a 6-figure business over time

- I recently created a program with a business partner to get books to the Wall Street Journal and USA Today bestseller lists and with just three clients, that brings us $100k in profits; so now I have multiple streams of six figure income.

- I have royalties from writing and publishing my own books, and this year (2020) I'm writing a book each month with the goal of having a 6-figure stream of income in 2021 from my books. I decided to do this because I read an article that said 6-figure authors have an average of 22-28 books published. Since I already had 10 books published, I decided I can add on 12 this year and be on my way to making six figures! The more books I write and publish, the more my passive royalty income increases!

I don't have all of these streams working at the same time, but typically for me I have at least four streams of income working at any given time; I think that's a good goal to set for yourself.

The key to creating multiple streams of income is that each income stream should not be restricted to certain hours. Especially if you have a 9-5 job or a regular full-time job. You need a freelance job you can do in your free time.

Let's brainstorm some ways you can start creating multiple streams of income. It's going to be a stretch if you've only had one stream of income your entire life and everyone around you does as well.

Before we brainstorm, I want to tell you a quick story about my assistant, Alex. He's been working for me since September 2019, and one of his tasks is to set up Amazon ads for my clients after a book launch. He is also a published author at 23 years of age. He left his 6-figure corporate job as a programmer and coder to travel the world and he has created multiple streams of income. One of those is working virtually for me.

Alex has become an expert at Amazon Ads and even created a program to set up 1000 ad campaigns on autopilot in clients' accounts in 24 hours.

Alex would initially set up ads for my clients, but the problem was these clients would never manage or monitor those ads so their books were becoming invisible on Amazon.

To keep a book on the bestsellers list and have visibility, you must have Amazon ads working 24/7 every day.

So I gave Alex permission to offer his services managing Amazon ads to my clients. Right now, he has about 20 clients paying $50 per month, per book. His goal is to have 167 paying clients because his goal is to create a 6-figure stream of income.

Brilliant! He saw an opportunity and he took it! I'm so proud of this young man because he has hustle, vision and he's a hard worker.

Because he has automated the process, he doesn't have to spend that time on each client. He manages and tweaks the ads, and the client's success is his success.

So now let's brainstorm some ways you can start creating multiple streams of income.

The fastest way to do this is to think about how you can monetize your current skillset. What skills do you have now that people would be willing to pay you for?

Go to **www.fiverr.com** and see all the ways people are making money as freelancers and you'll find some very interesting gigs. This will help you think outside the box.

Here are some fiverr gigs:

- Blog writing

- Writing a resume

- Sales copywriting

- Logo design

- Logo animation

- Flyer Design

- Brand Style Guides

- Illustration

- Business Cards and Stationary

- Character modeling

- Storyboards

- T-shirts & merchandise

- Car wraps

- Arts and crafts

- Canvas wall art design

- Jewelry creation

- Food illustration

- Pop up cards

- Game developing

- Cybersecurity

- Web design

- Ecommerce development

- Converting files

- Editing pictures

- Book cover design

- Personal finance

- Legal contract review

- Translation

- Video editing

- Video music

- Excel data entry

- Excel spreadsheet

- Relationship advice

There are thousands of ways for you to make money online. I like making money virtually because you don't physically have to go to an office or punch a time clock. You can do it in your spare time.

Another great way to start creating new streams of income is on **www.etsy.com** if you have the arts and craft gene. Here are some categories of things for sale on Etsy:

- Calligraphy

- Custom Pet Memorial Stone

- Handmade Soaps and Lotions

- Natural Hair Products

- Natural Hairbands

- Wall Decor

- Candles

- Vases

- Rugs

- Furniture

- Bedding

- Picture Frames

- Pillows

- Women's Clothing – Dresses, Tops, Skirts, Jackets, Sweaters, etc.

- Baby Clothing

- Baby and Toddler Toys

- Dolls and Action Figures

- Stuffed Animals

- Games and Puzzles

- Learning and School

- Kids Crafts

- Slime and Foam

- Wedding Decorations

- Baby Shower Decorations

- Birthday Decorations

- Drawing and Illustration

- Mixed Media and Collage

- Fiber Arts

- Dolls and Miniatures

You name it, someone is making it! Think about what talents and skills you have right now and there is probably an online platform available for you to sell your products or services on.

One of my favorite ways to make money (because I love to teach) is creating online courses. Instead of figuring out how to build your own website to sell an online course, you can use existing platforms such as:

- **Teachable**

- **Thinkific**

- **Ruzuku**

- **Udemy**

Years ago, when I first started my online business, I saw someone making six figures teaching guitar lessons online and thought that was amazing.

We live in a virtual world. Most people are busy and if they can learn or get what they need from the comfort of their home, then you can be the one to sell them what they need.

Pick one way you are going to add on a new stream of income and start taking action now! It's also fun because you can take all the income from this new stream to pay off your debt and start saving money so you can have one year's expenses in the bank soon.

I think a lot of people in corporate America are unable to use their creativity at their jobs, so they start a side hustle that's fun and creative to do!

My mom and I sold a variety of handmade arts and crafts back in the day at local craft shows that was a lot of fun.

You are only limited by your imagination.

Next, we are going to talk about learning *new* skills to pay the bills.

CHAPTER 9

NEW SKILLS TO PAY THE BILLS

"The beautiful thing about learning, is that nobody can take it away from you."

~ B.B. King

My mentor reminded me "Leaners are Earners" and I've always believed that the more I learn from reading books, taking online courses, hiring mentors and coaches, watching webinars, etc., the more money I will make.

I'm in love with learning and it has paid off for me.

It's easy to find a comfortable plot in life and camp out there for good. If you want to be a high income earner, you have to leave your familiar campsite.

In the book, *The End of Jobs*, by Taylor Pearson, he says:

"Today, a $40 internet connection and a free Skype account gives anyone access to the greatest talent pool in history. Instead of competing against the labor pool of a few hundred thousand or a few million people in your area near you for your job, you're competing against seven billion people around the world."

This means 7 billion people are your competition.

It's tough to get a job, even a low-skill, low-paying job. The competition is fierce.

I remember the days when you could walk into a business, fill out an application, and speak to someone about a job on the same day. That face-to-face connection and interaction has been replaced with technology, and it's very impersonal now.

We live in a virtual world and the people who get on board the technology train will not get run over by it.

The key is to learn as many skills as you can and begin monetizing those skills.

Here are some of the skills I learned over the years and monetized:

- Website Design

- Search Engine Optimization

- Book Publishing

- Microsoft Word, PowerPoint, and Excel

- #1 Bestseller Book Launches

- Writing books

- Sales

- I'm also an expert (self-taught) on a variety of software programs such as Aweber, Hootsuite, Leadpages, Amazon KDP and more

Learn & Earn

It's a great time to be alive! You can turn on your computer and learn almost anything from anywhere .

But before you sign up for a class, workshop, or coaching program, make sure that what you're signing up for is in high demand and that you will be able to execute on it and get paying clients.

I know so many people who took the "Life Coach" certification path, only to find out that they also need sales, technical, marketing, and branding skills. Anyone can go through a Life Coaching program and become certified, but what percentage of those people go out and make six figures or even make their money back.

It's easy to see only one side of the picture – the one you love (the fantasy one), but there is another side and that's the back end stuff that people don't think about.

Sample Before You Go All In

Pivot Planet (formerly named Vocation Vacations) is a website that allows you to find someone who is doing the job you want to do and consult with them to "test drive your dream job." I love that idea!

Go to the website and enter a description for the type of career or business you want to start and find an advisor that you can consult with.

Here are some featured advisor careers from their website:

- Voiceover Artist

- Blogger

- Filmmaker

- Technology Entrepreneur

- Airbnb host

- Marketing Firm Owner

- Professional Speaker

- Publisher

- Radio Personality

- Web Developer

- Online Course Creator

You can view the full list of advisors here: https://www.pivotplanet.com/browse

I recommend hiring an advisor so you can see if this is something you really want to do by learning the good, bad and ugly about it.

The biggest mistake people make is investing too much time, money and resources before making a dime on their business or idea.

Don't make that mistake. Hire an advisor and ask questions. If it's something that still interests you after that, then go out to the real world and make your first $1000 doing it. If you still love it after that, then you have the green light to invest more of your money, time and energy into it.

Here are ten questions you can ask your Advisor:

1. Does this job have the potential to make six figures?

2. How many hours do you spend on your business per week?

3. What do you love about your business?

4. What do you hate about your business?

5. What have you learned since you started this business that you wish you knew before you started?

6. Do I need any special training to do this and if so, what would you recommend?

7. How many years did it take for you to become successful?

8. What advice would you give to someone like me who is just starting out?

9. What were the three biggest mistakes you made in this business?

10. If you could do things over, would you choose this business again?

This will give you a good measure on whether this is really something you want to pursue.

If the business involves a lot of sitting at the computer, and you prefer to be outdoors, maybe that's not for you.

In 2011, I decided I wanted to learn the skill of website design. Not because I loved "website design" per se, but because I loved writing sales copy. Unfortunately, people don't search Google for copywriters, they search for website designers.

I decided the only way I could get paid to write the sales copy for websites was to learn how to build WordPress sites.

I signed up for a 6-week guided online course that cost me $297, and by the end of that course, I was making $2000-$6000 per month doing website design.

I loved many things about website design – the creativity, the writing, the branding, etc., but after a few years I decided it was not something I wanted to do forever, so I shut it down.

Website design is very labor intensive and somewhat frustrating because most people are not technical. It was a great way, however, to start generating extra cash. At the time, I needed that extra money to pay the bills and to give me more time freedom.

Remember, if you choose a skill to monetize, a business to start or a side hustle, it doesn't have to be your "forever" thing. It can simply be a means to an end – which is to pay off your debt, build a big stash of emergency cash and eliminate your money worries once and for all.

By all means, don't pick something you hate, but do your research and pick something that uses your natural talent and abilities. I chose website design and used a talent I already had—copywriting skills. Most people don't think about the sales copy of a website. They just hire a website design company and 9 times out of 10, they aren't copywriters. So the website ends up not converting visitors to customers.

Think about what skills interest you that you can learn and monetize. Here are some resources for you:

- **www.lynda.com** (which is now "LinkedIn Learning") is a great place to learn skills with a low time and monetary investment ($19.99/month or $29.99/month). They have over 760 courses you can sign up for. Here's one I found that looks amazing: https://www.lynda.com/Business-tutorials/Freelancing-Foundations/2825035-2.html

- **https://www.masterclass.com/all-access-pass** - the cost for masterclass is only $15 a month and there are some high-level teachers and courses on this platform.

- **https://www.udemy.com/** - The courses are priced individually, but they are not expensive. And I like that they have a rating system.

These three resources should help get you started.

If you have more money to invest, then you might consider hiring a private business coach.

When I wanted to take my online business to six figures, I hired an amazing business coach. I went from making a few thousand online to $22k per month in 90 days. I initially signed up for an 8-week program with him for $5k and then continued to pay $1k per month for ongoing coaching from 2014 to 2017. I attribute the help I received from my coach to my business success! It was worth the investment and more.

Before you hire a high-ticket coach, however, make sure you have the ability to execute on what you are hiring them to help you with.

Let me give you an example. An older couple hired me for my bestselling author program. As I began to work with them, I learned that they had signed up for a $10,000, 8-week program called "Clients on Demand" with Russ Ruffino. Unfortunately, they lacked the technical skills to actually implement what they learned. They wasted a lot of time and money.

Make sure you can execute what you're signing up for. Be radically honest with yourself. If you are very low-tech or tech-challenged, then don't sign up for a course to learn website design, etc.

The world is changing at a rapid pace, and if you think you can just keep doing what you've always done, you're going to find yourself unemployed, underemployed, and struggling for the rest of your life.

To get ahead and have financial freedom, you must start learning new skills that are in demand.

Next, we are going to talk about a skill that is not often taught – the skill of saving money!

PART 4 –
BE BRAVE & SAVE

"The habit of saving is itself an education; it fosters every virtue, teaches self-denial, cultivates the sense of order, trains to forethought, and so broadens the mind."

~ T.T. Munger

CHAPTER 10

THE AUTOMATIC MILLIONAIRE

"If you're financial plan is not on automatic, you will fail."

~ David Bach, Author of Automatic Millionaire

Having a budget, writing checks manually, transferring money from one account to another simply will not work because it requires you to be disciplined.

Rather than relying on memory, habit, and discipline, you can make your financial plan automatic!

Most people fail to save because they don't have the time or the discipline to make it happen.

It seems like the more we make, the more we spend. So it's easy to keep spending the money that we have coming in. When income increases, we keep increasing our spending. It's a vicious cycle.

Unfortunately, when you spend everything you make, you are going to have a life of stress, uncertainty, debt and fear.

Most people have less than three months' of expenses in savings because of all the small things we waste money on every day. We don't think about these small things, but that's what is draining away our cash.

In David Bach's book, *The Automatic Millionaire*, he talks about the Latte Factor and says that if you look at the average cost of a latte, it is approximately $150 per month ($5 x 7 days a week). If you invested that money and earned 10% interest, you would have almost $1 million dollars in 40 years.

I'm not telling you to give up your lattes, however, if you want to have an emergency stash of cash, then you must start looking at the small spending that is adding up and find better ways to make your money work for you.

Once you've made saving money a priority – which is the whole point of this book – then you will become much more aware of where your money is going and find new ways to reduce your expenses and increase your income.

LEARN TO PAY YOURSELF FIRST

We are so accustomed to paying ourselves last that it is going to require a huge paradigm shift.

People don't like budgets because they seem restrictive and they just aren't any fun!

We receive thousands of marketing messages every day to spend, spend, spend, so it's hard to get control of our spending. But the spending is eating away at your freedom and your future; that is the tradeoff.

When it comes to money, you want to be in control, not the creditors, the marketers, or the retailers – YOU!

Who is the first person we pay when we make money?

Uncle Sam of course! Then we pay the state taxes and of course, we have social security tax, Medicaid and unemployment. We end up paying 35 to 50 cents for each dollar we earn.

Did you know that up until 1943, the government did not take money out of your paycheck automatically? They waited until the following year for people to pay their income taxes. However, there was a big problem with this system. People just could not be counted on to budget well enough to put that money in reserves to pay the government.

So the solution was for the government to get paid first!

Now it's your turn to get paid first.

People who have become millionaires over time set up automatic deductions from their paychecks to go to things like IRA's, 401K's, Savings Accounts, automatic bill paying, etc.

Since they never see the money, it's out of sight, out of mind.

David Bach gives numerous examples of clients who became millionaires due to automating their finances.

He also talks about making an extra bi-weekly payment to your mortgage automatically and saving $119,000 on a $250k 30-year loan with an interest rate of 8%. That's a lot of savings.

One of the mistakes I made was having my checking and savings account in the same place. It was too easy to move money over to my checking account when I needed to pay a bill or decided to buy something impulsively.

With direct deposit, it is easier now than ever to have your money automatically deducted and sent to different accounts.

In his book, *Profit First: Transform Your Business from a Cash-Eating Monster to Money-Making Machine*, Mike Michalowicz has business owners set up five different accounts:

1. INCOME

2. PROFIT

3. OWNER'S COMPENSATION

4. TAX

5. OPERATING EXPENSES

Mike says, "The primary goal here is to establish a new automatic routine for you. I want the amounts to be so small you don't even feel them. The goal is to set up these automatic allocations immediately, and then adjust the percentages each quarter until we are aligned with our target distribution percentages. Take small easy steps and you will gain powerful momentum."

BABY STEPS

Why do most diets or exercise programs fail? Because people try to do too much all at once and then revert back to their old habits. Also, we spend a lot of time planning, reading, researching and not enough time executing.

THE AUTOMATIC MILLIONAIRE · 111

In his book, *Atomic Habits: An Easy & Proven Way to Build Good Habits & Break Bad Ones*, author James Clear says:

"It is easy to get bogged down trying to find the optimal plan for change: the fastest ways to lose weight, the best program to build muscle, the perfect idea for a side hustle. We are so focused on figuring out the best approach that we never get around to taking action."

Action delivers outcomes. That's it. So if you want to change your financial future, stop looking for the perfect approach and take action...but start out with small actions and work up to bigger ones.

Research shows that the more you repeat an activity, the more the structure of your brain changes to become efficient at that activity; so physical changes in your brain are happening as you repeat an activity.

It's easy to convince ourselves that we have to take massive action to have massive success, but here's how the math works out if you just focus on tiny improvements.

- Get better 1% each day for one year and you'll be 37 times better by the time you're done.

- Conversely, if you get 1% worse every day for a year, then you'll decline to zero.

Small changes at first seem barely noticeable, but over time, they can make a significant improvement in your life.

"Time magnifies the margin between success and failure."

So, tiny habits + automation + consistency = BIG results over time.

Results have very little to do with the goals you set and more to do with the systems you put in place. That's why both of these authors I mentioned above, suggest implementing automation to achieve the desired outcome.

In the book *Profit First*, the first order of business in the author's methodology is to "Cut Expenses." Next, "Destroy Your Debt" and finally, "Enjoy Saving More Than You Enjoy Spending."

If your paycheck stopped tomorrow, how long could you survive?

It's scary, right? I can survive two years without a paycheck, and I have learned to enjoy saving money more than spending it.

This is serious business because we live in an uncertain world and we need to be prepared to take care of ourselves and our families.

In the next chapter, I give you the action steps required to automate your finances and build a BIG Stash of CASH!

CHAPTER 11

THE BLUEPRINT TO BUILD A BIG STASH OF EMERGENCY CASH

The art is not in making money,
but in keeping it.

~ Proverb

In his book, *How to Live a Good Life,* author Jonathan Fields encourages people to think of their life in terms of three buckets:

1. The Vitality Bucket

2. The Connection Bucket

3. The Contribution Bucket

He explains, "The fuller your buckets, the better your life. When all simultaneously bubble over, life soars. That's what we're aiming for. But the flip side is also true. If any single bucket runs dry, you feel pain. If two go empty, a world of hurt awaits. If all three bottom out, you don't have a life."

I love his analogy to life and using the visuals of buckets.

Since this book is about finances, we are going to separate everything into four buckets:

1. The Debt Bucket

2. The Expenses Bucket

3. The Income Bucket

4. The Savings Bucket

There are dozens of ways to fill your financial buckets. In this chapter, I am going to suggest techniques you can use to fill your buckets. Many of these ideas and strategies, we discussed in earlier chapters.

The goal is to have enough emergency cash to be able to pay your bills for at least one year if something unexpected happened. When you get to that point, you will have peace of mind and the changes you make to get there will be worth the freedom and serenity you gain.

THE LAWS OF THE BUCKETS

Bucket Law #1: The bucket leaks – If the bucket is running dry, your job is to fill them as needed, never ignoring any of them long enough to run dry.

Bucket Law #2: An empty bucket will drag the others down with it – Essentially all buckets are connected, we can't abandon one bucket and hyper-focus on another. We need to give them all equal attention.

Bucket Law #3: The buckets never lie – If you have an empty bucket or leaking bucket, you will know.

Author and visionary thinker, Derek Sivers, says, "If information was the answer, then we'd all be billionaires with perfect abs."

Knowledge without action is meaningless. The blueprint provides steps for you to take to fill your buckets.

Let's get started with action steps for each bucket. Remember, just one action for each bucket right now is a step in the right direction. Don't get overwhelmed and feel like you have to do everything at once. Pick one thing in each bucket to do right now.

THE DEBT & CREDIT BUCKET

- Stop ordering online (except for necessities)

- Implement the 24-hour rule (or if that isn't long enough, make it the 48-hour rule before you spend over $100

- Set up baskets or file folders to save all your receipts. Once a month, review exactly where your money is going.

- Cut up or freeze your credit cards if you are using more than 30% of the credit limit.

- Consider connecting with Consumer Alliance if you are paying exorbitant amounts of interest and are maxed out.

- If you have a high car payment, consider refinancing at a lower rate or trading it for a lower priced more affordable car.

- Fill out the credit card chart in Chapter 6, and start paying off your cards; either with the highest interest first or the lowest balance. The key is to start. You can start doubling your payments with the extra money you have from lowering your expenses or also from creating new income streams.

- Pay off all your credit card debt if you are able to as soon as possible.

- Set up an account with Credit Karma and start tracking your credit score. Play the credit game and improve your score monthly. Remember, have no more than a 30% balance on a credit card and never pay only the minimum payment.

- Consider having a family member who has excellent credit, add you on to their credit card account as a user. Make sure they always pay on time and that you use the card and pay it off every month. This can significantly increase your credit score quickly. Verify that the bank or credit card company will report your new card to the credit bureau.

- If you've had to file bankruptcy or had a foreclosure or short sale and your credit is shot, apply for a secured credit card and make sure they report to the credit bureaus.

- Never have a maxed out credit card. If any of them are maxed out, you may need to consolidate or make additional payments to get them below the 30% mark. Or you can transfer to a zero percent interest card.

- Don't apply for a lot of credit in a short time period.

- Review all of your credit reports and request any derogatory information be removed.

THE EXPENSES BUCKET

Stay within these percentages for your living expenses:

- Giving 10%

- Food 10-15%

- Utilities 5-10%

- Housing 25%

- Transportation 10%

- Health 5-10%

- Insurance 10-25%

- Recreation 5-10%

- Personal Spending 5-10%

- Miscellaneous 5-10% (Savings will be in the Saving Bucket of at least 10% to start)

- Review all expenses and automatic payments and consider getting rid of some of the unnecessary ones.

- If you don't currently own a home, continue to rent until you are debt free and have one year of living expenses in a savings account. Remember how great it is NOT to have unexpected expenses or home improvement costs.

- If you own a home, consider refinancing it if you can get a lower interest rate; or sell your home and purchase a more affordable home if you have a high payment and are house poor.

- Renegotiate rates on cable services, cell phone services, internet services, lawn services, gas and electric utilities, service contracts, etc.

- Make a list of all of your current living expenses and see what you can eliminate.

- Review your bank statement for the past 90 days and see what money you spent on things not listed on your monthly living expenses list; this is where you leak money.

- Consider installing an app on your phone to track your spending and offset your unconscious spending habits.

THE INCOME BUCKET

- Sell any items in your house you aren't using, don't need, or overpaid for and put that money into your Savings Bucket. For example, you can go through all of your closes and take items you don't use or paid too much for to the consignment store and get cash for clothing, purses, coats, etc.

- Get a part-time gig selling; consider selling online – fiverr, etsy, or your own website. You can also be a sales consultant for other online business owners or an affiliate.

- Read as many books as you can about sales including books by Grant Cardone, Og Mandino, Donald Miller, and Jeffrey Gitomer

- Start one new stream of income as you move towards multiple streams of income; don't start anything that requires you to invest a lot of money at first. The goal is to increase your income, not your expenses.

- Learn new skills to pay the bills at Udemy, Masterclass or Linda.com.

- Consider creating an online course if you are tech savvy and use existing platforms such as Teachable, Thinkific, Udemy or Ruzuku.

- Sample a business/side-hustle/gig before you go all in by hiring a private advisor at pivotplanet.com and ask them the 10 questions I outlined in Chapter 9.

- Hire a private business coach; only if you have low debt and have at least 3-6 months savings in the bank; make sure to do your due diligence.

- Declutter your house. I believe that money doesn't come into a cluttered home or life. Start decluttering all your problem areas first and watch more money start flowing into your life.

- Don't bury your talents; share your talents with the world and soon you will be able to earn "play-checks" instead of "pay-checks."

THE SAVINGS BUCKET

- Pay yourself first – starting now you are going to put away 10% of your income (if you cut expenses and increase your income, you should have at least 10% to start with).

- Open a separate savings account at a different bank that you don't have easy access to and automatically set up direct deposits into this account if you can. Automation is key.

- Review your paycheck and see what deductions are coming out; before you put a lot of money into a 401k (which is very volatile right now), you should take that money and put it into your emergency cash stash.

- Research shows that people who use a tax professional or accountant end up getting back a refund on average of about $2000. My daughter did her taxes this year and determined she should receive an $1100 refund. She is a single parent and I thought she should be getting more than that back. I had my accountant do her taxes instead, and her refund now is $4500! I'm telling you, you're probably giving money to Uncle Sam that could be going right into your Savings Bucket.

- Clean out your closets and sell anything you have not worn or used in the past six months to one year; take that money and add it to your savings bucket.

- Your BIG emergency stash of cash is at least one years living expenses; calculate that now and put in writing how much should be in this account. Review that every day.

Slow and steady wins the race. Don't be naked when the tide goes out.

I want you to pick four action steps, one from each bucket that you are going to do in the next three days:

1. _____

2. _____

3. _____

4. _____

Remember, I had zero money in savings a year ago because I completely ignored and neglected my savings bucket. I was hyper-focused on making money, which is great, but not at the expense of ignoring my savings bucket.

My debt/credit bucket was doing well, my income bucket was excellent, my expenses bucket was mediocre, and my savings bucket was completely empty.

You must protect yourself and your family. Rainy day emergencies happen all the time and you must have at least one year's expenses in a savings account.

122 · MICHELLE KULP

Once you achieve that goal, you should aim for saving two years of living expenses.

Remember, the less you have to pay, the more you can play. We can live on so much less than we think we can; it's a matter of priorities and perspective.

The other day I was complaining to my daughter that the local restaurant didn't have my two of my favorite side dishes – creamed spinach and au gratin potatoes and her text back to me was *"First World Problems."*

She was absolutely right. What am I complaining about?

Mel Robbins, former attorney, life coach and host of the Mel Robbins talk show says we must change the language we use from "I have to" to "I get to" when we find ourselves complaining.

For example, I have to get another job to pay off this debt and start saving money can be turned into "I get to have another job to pay off this debt and start saving money."

"I have to pay off my debt" becomes "I get to pay off my debt."

We don't realize how lucky we are and how many options and opportunities are literally at our finger tips because of the internet.

Without the internet, I would still be working a 9-5 job in the legal field instead of working 20-25 hours a week, doing what I love, making six figures.

What you focus on grows. Focus on building up your savings using the buckets and you will be successful.

I believe in you and I believe that if you start now, in 12 months you can have at least six months living expenses in the bank, increase your income and decrease your debt!

Everything I shared with you is my personal story of how I went from zero in savings to $100k in one year. All it takes is a decision, commitment and action.

I believe in you!

CHAPTER 12

CLOSING THOUGHTS

"We are prone to confusing
excess with success."

Joshua Becker, author of The More of Less: Finding the Life You Want Under Everything You Own says:

"In America, we consume twice as many material goods as we did fifty years ago. Over the same period, the size of the average American home has tripled, and today that average home contains about three thousand items. On average, our homes contain more televisions than people. And the US Department of Energy reports that due to clutter, 25% of people with two-car garages don't have room to park cars inside and another 32% have room for only one vehicle…And one out of every ten American households rent off-site storage…No wonder we have a personal debt-problem. The average household's credit card debt stands at over $15,000 while the average mortgage is debt is over $150,000." (2015 statistics)

The bottom line is we own too much stuff. This book is a reminder that you will find more joy in owning less; by owning less, you will have less debt as well.

Consequently, having less debt, fewer expenses and less stuff, you will have more time, more money, less stress, less distraction, and most importantly, more FREEDOM.

Joshua Becker defines *Minimalism* in his book as "The intentional promotion of the things we most value and the removal of anything that distracts us from them."

The question is "What do you most value?"

For me, it is family, my time and freedom.

As you go down this path of working on your four financial buckets and as you start spending less money shopping and buying more things, you might find new benefits such as being able to travel more, retire earlier, make a much needed career change, move to a different home, and spend more time with family and friends.

If we aren't happy with our jobs or our lives, consumerism and buying things fills a void. Resisting consumerism gives us the possibility of finding real happiness when we are not in debt, are living within our means, and have a BIG stash of cash in savings.

Although I talked about starting with 10% savings because I believe in starting small and increasing that over time, the number I am aiming for personally is to save 50% of what I make.

It's time we define what success means for ourselves and forget about what others think. Admire success, but do not celebrate excess. Learning to tell the difference can change your life.

There have been times in my life where I was really good at saving money and then I would fall into the consumerism trap and start spending all my savings and living "fake rich," like when I purchased the million-dollar house with my ex-fiancé.

It might feel like you are putting yourself on a financial diet, but look at it this way – having debt and owning too much stuff is keeping you from freedom and happiness.

I 've learned that wanting the next best thing is a never-ending cycle. You want the newest iPhone, the newest car, the newest everything. It never ends.

Eckhart Tolle, in his book, *A New Earth: Awakening to Your Life's Purpose*, says:

"Ego is always identification with form, seeking yourself and thereby losing yourself in some form....I try to find myself in things but never quite make it and end up losing myself in them. That is the fate of the ego."

We can easily lose ourselves in materialism and consumerism until we wake up one day and we are completely miserable, have lost our purpose and our passion, and feel lost.

Eckhart says there are three dominant states of the ego:

1. Wanting

2. Thwarted wanting (anger, resentment, blaming, complaining)

3. Indifference

"Ego-identification with things creates attachment to things, obsession with things, which in turn creates our consumer society and economic structures where the only measure of progress is always MORE."

Ego satisfaction is always short lived and that is what keeps the consumer society going – you keep looking for more, keep buying and keep consuming.

As you become more aware of your choices and begin making better decisions, that will create a new financial future for you and your family, you will move away from making decisions from the dysfunctional ego and move toward making "awakened" decisions from your deep wisdom and connection.

I hope you have enjoyed this book. I find that I write books to teach myself things at a deeper level. So thank you for joining me on this journey to financial freedom and more conscious living.

With Much Love and Gratitude,

Michelle

ONE MORE THING

Can you do me a favor?

Before you go, I'd like to say thank you for purchasing my book. I really appreciate it!

I'd like to ask a small favor. Would you take a minute or two to leave a review for this book on Amazon?

This feedback will help me continue to write the kind of books that help inspire, motivate and educate people to believe in themselves and to find their true purpose in life.

If you enjoyed my book, then please let me know ☺

Michelle Kulp

www.ingramcontent.com/pod-product-compliance
Lightning Source LLC
Chambersburg PA
CBHW060612200326
41521CB00007B/749